# Technical Communication in the Information Age

Rebecca D. Snarski, Ph.D.
Capella University

*Copley Custom Textbooks*

An imprint of XanEdu Custom Publishing

**Copley Custom Textbooks**
An imprint of XanEdu Publishing, Inc.
138 Great Road
Acton, Massachusetts 01720
800-562-2147

# Contents

## Introduction

This book provides a foundation in technical communications, with a primary focus on written communications, but also including oral communications. The text provides a basic understanding of audience and writing purpose, as well as tips for writing well and credibly. Information is presented in such a way as to encourage the reader to consider how the basic tenants of good communications apply to their own writing. Rather than giving a set formula or a series of templates, this text seeks to help the reader learn how to adapt their own style to suit the needs of their specific writing project. See the contents for a complete overview. While this text focuses on communications for the information technology, computer science and engineering professional, its ideas are pertinent to most writers in any business or academic field.

**There is a unique aspect to this text which is important for the reader to understand, so please read this paragraph.** Throughout this text there are many principles of good writing presented and guidelines given. However, it is important to recognize that, just as with the English language, rules are made to be broken, and this text may seem to "break" some of the same guidelines that it describes. Essentially, this text seeks to help you learn to write in a way that is audience appropriate, one which helps your audience to grasp and remember what you write. Sometimes, to accomplish that goal you must bend or break some guidelines, as this text sometimes does. To help you understand how this concept is applied, and how the author chooses when to step outside of a guideline, this text has been footnoted. These footnotes draw your attention to specific instances where the author may seem to deviate from what is taught, to use a colloquialism, the footnotes will appear whenever the author seems not to practice what she preaches. Then, the footnote will briefly tell you **why** the author chose to deviate in this way. You can then judge for yourself whether such deviations are effective, or whether the author might have been better to stick with convention. Either way, these footnotes will help you to think about your writing more deeply, and to consider how you can be flexible in your writing to ensure that your documents accomplish their purpose and suit their audience.

## Acknowledgements

This book was years in the making, slowed down by the distraction of a dissertation that needed to be completed as well as the daily rigors of life. Through those years my friends and family all helped to encourage and prod me. Thanks to my parents for their ever present support and faith, to Scruffy for letting me make this a priority, and for drinking Orange Crush, and to John "Odie" for braving the dangerous gulf-crabs to wrangle bottles. Thanks to Karen Mauck for her excellent editing skills and prompt attention, to Bill Akins for his help in providing a reality check on content and a sounding board for ideas, and to Jill Hackett for her thoughtful input. Thanks to Steve Gruchawka, Mark Jankowski and Marty Snarski for the use of their work as examples. And thank you to everyone at Capella University who supported me and helped me to get this text completed and published.

## About the Author

Dr. Rebecca Dawn Snarski holds a Bachelor of Arts in Public Relations and Promotion Management from the University of Alaska Fairbanks, a Master of Science in Communications Technology and a Ph.D. in Education from Capella University. Rebecca has been working in communications and technical writing for over twenty years, developing documents from press releases and advertisements to automotive service manuals, Web sites and journal articles. Rebecca has written documents for such companies as AMC Theaters, Capella University, DaimlerChrysler, Ford and General Motors. In her personal time Rebecca enjoys creative writing projects, and has written an unpublished screenplay and two teleplays, as well as various short stories.

Rebecca splits her time between Tampa, Florida, and Port Huron, Michigan, where she lives with her partner, their young son, and three cats.

# CHAPTER 1

# Introduction to Technical

# Communications

---

*Whenever we have an experience that seizes upon
our imagination we find inevitably in the experience itself
the impulse to communicate it.*
*~Earle*

# Chapter 1: Introduction to Technical Communications

## The Information Age

The term Information Age is used to describe our current society, one in which the creation, manipulation and dissemination of information is paramount. Some argue that the developed countries of our planet entered the Information Age in the 1980s, when businesses dedicated to handling information became more prominent than those dedicated to manufacturing or other physical labor. Others mark the change in tide to an Information Age back even further, perhaps as far as the late 1800s, with the invention of the telegraph and telephone. Whenever one marks the beginning, there is no argument that today we live in a globally connected, information-based society – the Information Age is in full swing, with information-based business growing at a steady rate.

We could spend paragraphs, even pages, discussing the myriad ways that information is ever-present in our world, from voice-over internet protocol telephone service to e-mail, but you know as well as the author that communications is everywhere, and that communications and information-based businesses are all around us. So, let's look instead at information itself. What is information?

The American Heritage Dictionary defines information as:

1. Knowledge derived from study, experience, or instruction.
2. Knowledge of specific events or situations that has been gathered or received by communications; intelligence or news.
3. A collection of facts or data; statistical information (2007)[1].

Essentially, information refers to raw facts and data – knowledge in a basic form before any interpretation. In most cases, simple information itself is not particularly useful to a person or company, not until it has been evaluated and presented in a meaningful way. That is where communications comes in – communications is a means to disseminate information in a useful, meaningful way.

## Defining Technical Communications

Technical communications is a broad term, encompassing many different types of communications and expanding into various fields. Every professional in today's Information Age, no matter their field, is required to communicate with others at some time or in some way, whether written or oral.  These types of professional communications fall under the umbrella of technical communication. As much as the world seems to be changing to make face-to-face interaction obsolete, it is interesting to note that the communications industry is growing at an unprecedented rate.

Technical communications was once considered the responsibility only of those with the job title of technical writer or editor. Companies that needed owner's manuals for their products would hire technical writers, who usually were not engineers, to create such information. Even automotive companies used non-technical employees who specialized

---

[1] Note that the author has chosen American Psychological Association (APA) format for citing references. The citation of references is important in any writing, as will be discussed in future chapters.

in writing to create user and service materials. But this would sometimes cause problems; information was often miscommunicated and documents could be technically unclear. Recently, a trend has begun where engineers and technical specialists are actually creating documentation, or at least more closely proofing the work of writers. In the business workplace, a similar trend is happening. No longer are letters, memos, reports and other written materials created exclusively by secretaries or assistants. With the proliferation of computers and other communication advances, more workers, team leaders, managers and CEOs are creating their own communications documents than ever before.

Technical communications can be part of many modern jobs, particularly in the field of information technology. Among the professionals called upon to communicate technical information at some point in their careers are Web developers, programmers, engineers, visual design specialists, usability professionals, network specialists, instructional designers, teachers and trainers, content developers and network security managers. So, while technical communications was originally considered to include only product specifications, owner's manuals and other technical information, it eventually came to include business communications such as press releases, memos, annual reports and research projects and now includes Web page text, white papers, proposals, progress reports, evaluations and even e-mails. Essentially anything that is written or presented for a professional purpose is considered technical communications, and most professionals are at some time called upon to create such communications. Furthermore, the global nature of business today necessitates frequent communications between offices and persons in other cities, states and even countries. Phone conferences and e-mail proliferates, and it is incredibly important that these types of communication be clear and free from confusion.

## The Importance of Technical Communications

It is impossible to overestimate the importance of clear, concise, effective communications, particular in written form. From cavemen drawing on walls to Egyptian hieroglyphics to the modern press, writing has started wars, freed slaves and accomplished such impossible tasks as helping us all hook up our high-tech stereo systems. But unclear writing can cause as many problems as clear writing can solve.

Let us look at one powerful example of beautiful and life-altering writing that is at times both clear and effective, as well as obscure and unclear. Think for a moment about the United States Declaration of Independence. If asked to recite a portion of the Declaration, those of you who could would likely begin with the following quote:

> We hold these truths to be self-evident, that all men are created equal, that they are endowed by their Creator with certain unalienable Rights, that among these are Life, Liberty and the pursuit of Happiness (U.S. Government, 1776, ¶2)[2].

These words are strong, meaningful, and for many, form the cornerstone of the United States. They are also relatively easy to understand, even if words such as "self-evident," "endowed" and "unalienable" are not words that are commonly used in modern English.

---

[2] This type of quote, set off by indenting of every line, but without quotation marks, is used in APA format and is called a "block quote."

The meaning is clear: all men are equal and have the rights to life, liberty and happiness. But consider the ramifications if this had been reworded slightly.

Even minor rewording can make a dramatic difference in a document. At the time of the creation of the Declaration of Independence, slavery was a common practice in the colonies. Consider our history if the Declaration's lead writer, Thomas Jefferson, had instead written, "that all white men are created equal." Or, "that all citizens are created equal." Perhaps, "all land-owners are created equal." Maybe even, "that all men, white and colored, are created equal." If you think about it, the word "men", to the apparent exclusion of women, has been a source of dispute for over two hundred years; the omission or addition of just one word can change the meaning of an entire document, and could, realistically, have changed history. The pen is truly a powerful tool, or weapon.

Above we discussed the second paragraph, also called the preamble, of the Declaration. Did you know that was the *second* paragraph, not the first? How many of us could recite any portion of the first paragraph? Well, let's take a look at it this first paragraph, also called the introduction:

> When in the Course of human events, it becomes necessary for one people to dissolve the political bands which have connected them with another, and to assume, among the powers of the earth, the separate and equal station to which the Laws of Nature and of Nature's God entitle them, a decent respect to the opinions of mankind requires that they should declare the causes which impel them to the separation (U.S. Government, 1776, ¶1).

After reading this, consider why most of us can not recite this first verse. Is it any less poetically written than the preamble? Not really. The language is beautiful and elegant. However, the content is less compelling, and the language is less clear. This paragraph says, essentially, that when a country wants to break free from the rule of another they should list, in writing, the reasons why. That's it. Not that exciting when compared to the preamble, but an important introduction to set the reader's expectation for the document. Not only is the paragraph a bit less exciting, it is also more difficult to read. If you examine the paragraph, it seems that the statement, "When in the Course of human events," could simply be shortened to "When." Perhaps this would be more clear, but it would not fit the verbose language of the time, nor have the elegance of the remaining document. Similarly, you could revise the rest of this paragraph and probably break it down to one brief, concise line.

You might ask, "Interesting, but what is the point?" Well, it's this: that writing is not a science. Rather, it is an art form, but an art form that can be learned. A good writer learns to balance words in a way that captures and maintains interest, while also communicating clearly, concisely and effectively. Sometimes there are valid reasons to use over-the-top, colorful language. Other times it is wise to consider every word carefully and be as clear and succinct as possible. As a communicator, it is up to you to decide what is called for in your situation. Throughout this book, you will explore different aspects of communications, and in the end it will be your responsibility to put together what you learn, each time you write, into a package appropriate to your current purpose and audience.

**Shuttle Disasters**

Now let us look at one compelling example of the importance of good communications and the danger of inadequate communications: the United States Space Shuttle program.

On January 28, 1986, NASA made the decision to launch the Space Shuttle Challenger, despite reservations voiced by certain engineers as to the ability of the o-rings to function properly in the cold temperatures projected for the morning of the launch. Just seconds after launch the o-rings failed and the shuttle exploded, killing the entire crew and shocking the nation.

While there were many factors that contributed to the loss of Challenger, communications played a major role. In short, when preparing to launch the Challenger Shuttle flight 51-L, there was concern among a number of Morton Thiokol engineers that the o-rings used on the solid rocket boosters had shown a potential for failure when tested during cold temperatures (Rogers Commission, 1986). Various engineers sent multiple memos for years before the launch, warning of the potential failure. Reports show that the memos were mostly dismissed as speculation or not routed to the correct person (Rogers Commission). The situation illustrates two problems – the unwillingness of management to listen to their engineers, and the inability of the engineers to push an important point to the forefront.

The night before the Shuttle launch, a number of Morton Thiokol engineers became gravely concerned. After escalating their concerns, they participated in a telephone conference between Morton Thiokol and Marshall Space Flight Center management (Rogers Commission).  During this first conference, the engineers explained the potential for the o-rings to fail under cold conditions. They did not have hard numbers, and, according to some records, perhaps did not get their point across.

Shortly after the shuttle disaster President Regan formed the Presidential Commission, also called the Rogers Commission, to investigate. During the Rogers Commission investigation, participants in the above mentioned telephone conference from Marshall Space Flight Center were asked, "So as early as after that first afternoon conference at 5:45, it appeared that Thiokol was basically saying delay. Is that right?" (Rogers Commission, Chapter 5). One member replied, "That is the way it came across to me." But another person, attending the same conference, replied, "I did not perceive it that way. I perceived that they were raising some questions and issues which required looking into by all the right parties, but I did not perceive it as a recommendation delay" (Rogers Commission, Chapter 5).

The Rogers Commission learned that later the same day a second telephone conference was held. For this conference, the Morton Thiokol engineers presented charts and data illustrating o-ring performance in various temperatures. Some management questioned the data, and the engineers admitted that it was incomplete and that the o-rings had not been tested specifically at the anticipated flight temperature. However, the engineers, as reported in the Commission review, specifically advised that the lift-off should be delayed. In the end, management decided that, given the fact that the o-ring in question was a secondary o-ring and that the data was not confirmed, launch would commence. Upon launch, the primary seal failed, as did the secondary seal, resulting in the complete loss of the Shuttle Challenger.

Upon completion of their investigation, the Rogers Commission found that, "Marshall Space Flight Center project managers, because of a tendency at Marshall to management isolation, failed to provide full and timely information bearing on the safety of flight 51-L to other vital elements of Shuttle program management" (Rogers Commission, Chapter 9, V). In addition, it was found that communications is not just about sending, or even about receiving. It is also about the communications climate, and the willingness of participants to listen to those whose opinions they solicit. Thus, the Rogers Commission further stated that, "The nation's reliance on the Shuttle as its principal space launch capability created a relentless pressure on NASA to increase the flight rate. Such reliance on a single launch capability should be avoided in the future" (Chapter 9, VIII). Essentially, NASA was working in a political and business climate that left little room for action that was contrary to that which was planned[3].

There is no one person or even one group to blame for the shuttle disaster. Rather, there were various incidents of inadequate communications, communications that were either unclear, misrouted, unsupported or untimely. There was also a lack of receptiveness on the part of the management. A climate existed that made postponing the launch a negative decision, and thus closed the minds of the Marshall Space Flight Center management to various issues that were presented. This is an effective, if sad, reminder that communications is a two-way street; a communicator must disseminate clear, concise, understandable information, and receivers must be open to what they are being told.

Seventeen years and 88 shuttle launches later, on February 1, 2003, tragedy struck again as the Columbia Shuttle flight 107 broke up on re-entry into the Earth's atmosphere due to damage sustained upon launch. During launch of the Columbia, a piece of foam insulation broke free from the main propellant tank, striking the leading edge of the left wing and damaging the tile, part of the Shuttle's thermal protection system. Upon re-entry, the heat build-up caused the destruction of the shuttle.

The Columbia Accident Investigation Board (CAIB) embarked on a large-scale investigation to determine the cause of the disaster and make recommendations for the future. The Board reported that, "the NASA organizational culture [the basic values, norms, beliefs and practices] had as much to do with this accident as the foam" (CAIB, 2003, "Introduction"). Specifically, the commission felt that after the Cold War ended in the 1980s NASA lost much of its funding, and thus to stay profitable had to increase their launches while decreasing their costs. This, reportedly, lead to an atmosphere that left room for mistakes, such as Columbia.

According to CAIB, concerns over the foam and tile had been expressed prior to the Columbia launch. However, similar to the Challenger disaster, the communications on the issue were not timely or specific, and management, given the political climate of NASA, was not willing to listen. The CAIB agreed with the Rogers Commission that failures in communications, incomplete and misleading information and poor decisions allowed these shuttles to launch when they should not have[4].

---

[3] You can read the complete Rogers Commission report, on the NASA Web site (http://history.nasa.gov/rogersrep/v1ch1.htm).
[4] You can read the complete CAIB report on NASA's Web site (http://spaceflight.nasa.gov/shuttle/archives/sts-107/investigation/index.html).

As the Rogers Commission concluded, "The Commission applauds NASA's spectacular achievements of the past and anticipates impressive achievements to come. The findings and recommendations presented in this report are intended to contribute to the future NASA successes that the nation both expects and requires" (Chapter 9, "Concluding Thoughts"). Similarly, through this discussion the author wishes in no way to disparage the amazing accomplishments of NASA and the value of the United States' Space Program, but seeks to draw attention to the much-needed changes in the communications policies of the program and to illustrate that effective communications can, in fact, be life altering.

**Summary**

While incomplete, poorly written or ill-timed communications can cause myriad problems in any organization, effective communications can be of great benefit. A properly written document can save you, as the writer, time by eliminating the need for your audience to offer questions or for you to continually update and clarify your thoughts. Effective writing saves time for a reader by allowing them to immediately understand what is being communicated and eliminate the need for further research or questions on the topic.

Effective writing is more likely to serve its intended purpose, whether you are trying to instruct readers on assembly of their new entertainment cabinet, trying convince a college instructor that you have understood the concepts in class or asking your boss for a raise. Good communications skills, both written and oral, are important soft-skills that you, as an employee, bring to the workplace. Such skills are highly valued by employers in every field, but especially in information technology. They are also valuable skills for your academic career and your personal life.

As you read the rest of this book, be an active reader. Look for pieces of information that you can use. Consider how the ideas presented fit into your workplace, academic career or personal life, or how they may in the future.

# CHAPTER 2

# Audience and Purpose

---

*It is better that the grammarians should chide us than that the people should not understand us.*
*~Pei*

# Chapter 2: Audience and Purpose

## Introduction

Audience and purpose are the two most important considerations when writing a document. If you do not understand who your audience is, and recognize their level of knowledge, you cannot communicate with them in a meaningful way. If your document has no defined purpose, then it will accomplish nothing.

Audience is of paramount importance because without an audience you would not need to write anything – there would be no one to use or care about your document. Similarly, if you do not write in a way that is audience appropriate, your point may be lost upon your reader, and thus your document will not be useful to those for whom it is intended.

Purpose is an important aspect of writing, as you obviously need a reason for creating a document. Sometimes you might be writing a document that is intended to serve a single purpose, sometimes multiple purposes; either way, if your document does not properly address what it is supposed to, does not serve its intended purpose, then it is meaningless[5]. As you read this text, consider the reasons why you have written or may write in the future, the audiences that you have or will write for, and how what you read may apply to your writing.

## Audience

When thinking about your audience, there are a number of variables to consider. For example, you might consider the following questions:

- Is there a single, specific audience who will be interested in your work, or will it be for a diverse audience?
- What is the background, knowledge level and expectations of the intended reader?
- What assumptions might they make or what feelings might they have before reading your document?
- What assumptions do **you** have about your audience?

Anticipate what questions your specific audience will have. Consider what they already know, what they want to know and what they may not even realize they need to know. If you are writing to an audience that is eager to read your work, this can be easier. But if you are writing to a less interested audience, you may have to work harder to ensure that you grab and hold their interest to accomplish your task. For example, if you are writing a text book for a middle school computer class, chances are your audience feels they know what they need to about computers, and is less than eager to read your work. In a case like this, you will want to make an extra effort to write in a way that is

---

[5] This text does not include a section on grammar and punctuation. though in Unit 3 it will refer you to such texts. However, the author would like to point out one punctuation issue here, as it is a commonly misused punctuation – the semi-colon. Note that a semi-colon is usually used to separate two clauses that are actually two grammatically complete sentences (that is, they could each stand alone) but where their ideas or topics are so inter-related that the writer wishes to connect them directly, so instead of making them two separate sentences, the writer uses a semi-colon. You will see this used often throughout this text.

interesting, perhaps even humorous, and particularly relevant to what interests your audience[6].

Before you embark on a writing project, you must KNOW your audience. You must recognize who they are before you begin writing. Then, after you are done writing, you should read your work, placing yourself in the audience's shoes, and be certain that you wrote in a language they will understand and appreciate.

## Purpose

The purpose of a document is generally to persuade, teach, or inform. You might write a proposal, trying to persuade your boss to change your computers over to the newest operating system. You might write a manual to teach people how to use your software. You might write a paper to inform your stockholders about the financial status of the company. Or, you might write a paper that does all of these things. But you MUST have a clear purpose in mind in order to write your paper effectively. You should also consider your own motivations when writing, thinking about why you want to write on a specific topic, or what is driving you. This can help you work out the details of your purpose. Know what you are trying to accomplish, and as you write, occasionally reevaluate to ensure that you are heading in the right direction, including the necessary information and using the proper tone.

One example of a specific purpose might be if you are writing something that you know will be translated into another language. Most of us have read DVD or stereo instructions that tell us, "Put the cord onto the left utmost hole in the unit." You know these instructions were not originally written in English. Perhaps you have been charged with writing a company report that you know will be translated and sent to your parent company out of the country. You should begin by asking yourself how you can, as the writer, make it easier for such writings to be translated properly. The most important considerations in such situations actually can apply to almost all writing. When writing for potential translation, one should use grammatically complete language that is clear, concise and free from slang or words that have dual meanings. As you write, consider what other restrictions might apply to your writing based on the various purposes of the document.

## Other Concerns

One other major consideration in writing is the guidelines, parameters or framework that you are writing within. This, in a way, is a sub-set of the audience and/or purpose considerations. For example, if you are writing a magazine article, you may be told that you are being given space for 1,500 words – no more, no less. Thus, length becomes an important parameter, or constraint, for you to write within. If you are writing a technical manual for a new product that your company is producing, you might be told that you have to have the manual completed and ready to ship with the product on the product release date; thus the timeline becomes an important parameter. Any guideline or requirement that you are given should be kept in mind throughout development of your document. It is important to follow such rules and guidelines if you are to satisfy the

---

[6] This text, in fact, is written in a very casual tone, using contractions, second person "you" statements and occasionally even some slang to make reading easy, and hopefully more enjoyable, for the audience.

customer you are writing for, especially if that customer is the person who signs your paycheck or assigns your course grade.

## Maintaining Audience, Purpose and Guidelines

When you are about to embark on the development of a document, take a moment to reflect upon the audience for your writing, the purpose of the document, and any guidelines, requirements or restraints. It is a good idea to start your paper with a few notes at the top that you can refer back to as you work (but be sure to delete these when you are finished). For example, say you are taking a class to improve your skills in computer network security. One of your assignments is to write a brief paper on biometrics, the use of fingerprints, retinal scans and other physical traits to verify identification.

You might begin by starting a new word processing file, then putting a working title at the top of your paper (you can always tweak the title later, but it helps to start with something). Then, you would add some basic information to help guide you as you write. In the beginning, you may start with something similar to Figure 2.1.

---

Biometrics: The Future of Information Security

Audience: Course instructor, familiar with IT and security, and fellow students with varying levels of IT knowledge.

Purpose: To overview the basics of biometrics for a novice audience.

Guidelines: Required to cite references in APA format.
Must use at least 4 different sources.
Must be exactly 10 pages in length.
Must use at least 4 graphics in paper, properly labeled.
Due March 31st.

---

Figure 2.1: Starting File

From here, you begin writing your paper. As you complete sections of your paper and begin proofreading and fixing them, occasionally refer back to these notes to ensure that you are meeting all requirements and writing in a way that is appropriate to your audience and purpose.

When you are finished with the paper, or just before the final stages of proofreading, delete your notes, finalize your title and fill out the remainder of your paper header (name, date, etc.).

## Communicating with Different Populations

The United States has always been a nation of diverse cultures, people and customs. More and more our society is moving toward increasing diversity, in our schools, our social circles and in business. America is becoming more global as companies open branches around the globe, international trade continues to grow, immigration booms and communication technology allows us to communicate around the world in an instant. As mentioned previously, many of the documents that we write will be used by people for whom English is a second (or third) language, or they may be translated into foreign languages. The sheer volume of global communications in today's world, from business memos to personal e-mail and even international sales on public sites such as eBay, work to increase the potential for cross-cultural miscommunication.

Cultural interactions and mixing is not limited to metropolitan areas or major cities. Even in our more rural areas, it is practically impossible for any American not to interact with people different from themselves on a daily basis. This brings about the potential for misunderstandings and miscommunications, particularly when we lack knowledge about the customs of those who are culturally different than ourselves. Of course, no one can be forced to learn to live in our diverse world, but those who do learn are more likely to reap the rewards. Understanding, or at least respecting, the differences between various people and cultures can help to improve human relations and quality of living, increase our feelings of safety and lead to financial benefits from business contacts. In the business world, catering to different audiences and customer bases and responding to the needs of various clients, patients, customers and others with whom we interact can pay off in myriad ways.

Communicating effectively across social, racial and cultural lines is one of the most difficult tasks many business professionals face today. But it is important to remember that the majority of civilized people have a similar set of values; we value education, civil harmony, good job performance, valuable skill development, truthfulness and responsibility. Learning to communicate in and with groups different than ourselves is paramount to our personal and business success. Understanding the differences in communication styles is the first and most important step to overcoming this obstacle.

When trying to communicate with a specific group of people who are different from you, it is important to get to know that group a bit. Certainly, you must remember that every group is not homogenous – you cannot fall prey to stereotypes that place specific labels onto certain groups by their race, gender, religion, orientation or such. But there are some general attributes of a society that you can consider. Research shows that the gay population, on average, is highly educated and upper middle class. This can make them an attractive marketing group. Experience tells us that women, even in today's modern world, purchase most household cleaning products; this provides valuable information for those working in this field. When you are trying to reach a specific audience, learn about them – where they live, what they read, how much money they earn. Remember that stereotypes are seldom based in reality, but that demographics and other research can show valuable trends to help you understand and better communicate with your audience.

Learning to communicate effectively with mixed audiences involves a number of different strategies and guidelines, as discussed in the next section.

## Communicating to a Mixed Audience

Communicating with different types of people can be challenging. Whether the differences are cultural, gender or age based or a result of other social or demographic differences, there are always things to take into consideration. It is important to communicate clearly to your audience, ensuring that they understand your words and meaning, but it is also important to communicate in a way that is not rude, unpleasant, condescending or otherwise negative. The best way to ensure that you communicate properly is to learn about your audience, understand them and what makes them unique, what needs they have, what tendencies and communication issues they have.

Cultural background can affect many facets of a person's personality and actions. It can affect ideas of what is on time, what is early and what is late. Cultural or religious differences can affect what dates are considered of importance or which are observed as holidays. Culture can impact the level of familiarity and informality that is used and expected in personal interaction, and it can affect the language and idioms that one uses and understands. It is important that you, as a communicator, learn to understand such variations in your audience. To effectively communicate with a specific group of people learn how time is managed in their culture, what holidays could be an issue to your deadlines, and, when communicating in a live context, how best to use body language.

### Language

The most basic guideline to communicating in culturally diverse situations is to be particular about the language you choose. Be clear, concise, yet complete. Explain things clearly, but without speaking at a level that is beyond the audience's understanding. Avoid the use of slang terms or Americanized expressions[7]. One often related story is of an immigrant worker who refused a much-needed job because he was told that it was on the 'graveyard shift,' and he assumed that meant he would be working in a cemetery. If you are talking to an English as a Second Language (ESL) speaker and you suddenly receive a blank look consider the idea that you might be using an expression that the person does not understand and try rephrasing.

If you are writing something that will be used in another country, or even something that may be translated, it is important, as mentioned previously, to take care to choose the correct words. Some words in English have counterparts of similar sound or spelling in other languages, but very different meanings. For example, a popular U.S. made car in the 1980s was the Chevrolet Nova. When the car was originally sold in Mexico, sales were painfully low. As it turns out, Nova is very similar to the Spanish phrase "no va," which means "it doesn't go." Who would buy a car that does not go? Even countries that speak the same language can have very different slang words. For example, in the United States in the 1990s "Free Willy", a children's movie about a killer whale in captivity, was a great hit, but the movie was a joke when first released in England because in England "willy" refers to a certain part of the male anatomy. To aid in translation avoid slang and idiomatic expressions. In graphics that will be used in foreign documents, avoid putting words in the actual graphic; rather, use symbols, then provide a key. That way, only the key needs to be changed for translation.

### Style

Remember that not all cultural groups view graphics, colors or shapes in the same way. "Universal" symbols are not always universal – what means one thing in one language

---

[7] Just an interesting aside, in an early draft of this text this line read, "Explain things clearly, but without speaking over a person's head." Then an editor pointed out that this was, in fact an idiom, which might not be appropriate to all audiences.

may mean something completely different in another. It is similar for color; in Japan white flowers symbolize death, whereas in Mexico purple flowers symbolize death. Shapes, gestures and body language may also have very different meanings for different people. One example is the "thumbs up" symbol, common in American culture. This is a friendly, positive gesture in American culture, indicating agreement or appreciation. However, in some Middle Eastern countries, among others, it is a highly offensive gesture.

Formality and informality are another part of style that varies from culture to culture. What one group finds acceptable might be appalling to another. Many Asian and other countries hold teachers in very high esteem, and to call a teacher by their first name would be gravely disrespectful. In other cultures, to call anyone older than you by their first name is disrespectful. Yet in America, many younger women are offended when called "Ma'am", as they feel it denotes an older age.

### Overcoming Barriers

There are no right or wrong ways to communicate with people of diverse backgrounds or cultures, but following are some good general guidelines to make communications easier and more productive:

- Avoid slang or technical jargon.
- Be concise and to the point, yet clear and specific.
- Spell out or say completely all acronyms the first time that you use them, even those that you think are common.
- Ask for feedback, ensure that you are understood, and respond to any feedback accordingly.
- Anticipate what questions your audience might have.

There are hundreds, even thousands, of variations in communication styles in the world. If you take the time to research the backgrounds and customs of your audience and show respect for their beliefs and opinions, you can ensure that your writing suits your audience and thus accomplishes your purpose with credibility. Communicating effectively with an audience means trying to use the language of your audience or a language that they will understand.

## Summary

In our increasingly global world, learning to communicate with people of varying backgrounds, beliefs and cultures is paramount in any business. Communicating with different types of people can be challenging. Whether the differences are cultural, gender or age based or a result of other social or demographic differences, there are always things to take into consideration. Whether communicating directly or through writing, with diverse audiences, there are a few guidelines that you can use to make your message more clear, as follow:

- Avoid slang words.
- Be concise, yet specific.
- Spell out all acronyms the first time they are used.
- Ask for feedback, and give that received due consideration.

In general, when working in and with diverse communities, it is important not only to respect the people with whom you are working, but also to learn how to best to utilize their diversity as a resource and leverage it to improve your group or businesses productivity.

# CHAPTER 3

# Credibility through Ethics

# and Mechanics

---

*The difference between the right word and almost
the right word is the difference between
lightning and lightning bug.*
*~Mark Twain*

# Chapter 3: Credibility through Ethics and Mechanics

## Introduction

As was discussed in previous chapters, for writers to be effective they communicate to the audience in an appropriate way, with an understanding of their audience and the purpose of the communication. However, effectiveness in writing is also dependant upon the ability of the writer to convince the reader that what they are reading is worthy of their attention – that it is credible. Credibility is important in every type of writing. For example, if you are writing a white paper (a type of professional paper that argues a position or problem) or proposal, you are likely trying to convince your reader of something or explain something in great detail. Your reader will be more likely swayed to your point of view if they perceive you as a credible source of information.

As you read through this chapter, pause to think about how the concepts of credibility apply to you in your professional life. Consider whether you have recently read documents you felt were not credible. If so, think about how they could have been written better, in a way that made you trust their content more. Or if you have recently read something that you felt was credible, consider what the author did to make you feel that way.

## Credibility

Projecting credibility in writing is sometimes done explicitly, by actually telling the reader why the writing, or more specifically the writer, is credible. For example, magazine and journal articles, as well as books and Web sites, often tell a bit about the author, detailing their educational degrees and their experience, and explicitly explaining to the reader why they should give credence to the assertions of the author.

Credibility can also be illustrated indirectly, simply through writing in a way that is engaging, professional, accurate and, when necessary, objective, as well as firm. A writer does this through the use of proper format, strong grammar and vocabulary and solid writing style. It is a matter of showing, rather than telling – simply appear credible, and you are more likely to be viewed as credible. Consider it the grammatical version of dressing for success; if a document looks good, it is more likely to be accepted.

While we put much emphasis on writing in this text, communications is certainly not limited to the written word. Most of what is covered in this book applies to the oral word, as well as written. How you speak is important, whether you are applying for a communications job or a data entry position. Would you hire someone whom you were interviewing for a receptionist job if they said "ain't" in every other sentence? Maybe, if they were going to be selling hot dogs, or if they were going to be working in computer lab, never having contact with customers. Likely not if they were going to be working in a law firm or a telephone help desk and interacting with clients – that kind of language just does not sound very professional. And certainly you would not hire them if there were other candidates who were just as qualified and also spoke better English.

Your academic and work-related writing should reflect your verbal grammar, and both should be professional and proper as well as reflect upon your position as an IT or business professional. This does not mean that you have to speak perfectly, but it means that you may have to learn to get past your years of habitual grammatical errors, learn to spell check and learn to speak and write in a way that makes people want to listen to you. This is type of proper oral and written grammar is also important in academic settings.

## Grammar and Mechanics

Grammar texts abound; you can find dozens of them on the shelves of any bookstore, and literally hundreds at online booksellers. In general, one grammar book is as good as the next; each will present you will lists of rules for using punctuation and corresponding examples. Most will have discussions of common grammar errors, commonly confused words and more. For a brief list of grammar books that this author finds particularly well written or useful see the end of this chapter. In our reading here, we will not discuss specific grammar rules, but instead present a number of basic guidelines to bear in mind when writing.

Grammar, punctuation and sentence structure are ways that you give an impression of credibility. Following is a list of common grammatical and structure issues/rules of which you should be aware:

- Avoid contractions in academic and professional writing.
- Be consistent with verb tenses.
- Avoid the passive voice, unless necessary to your specific purpose (Note that academic writing often requires you to write in passive voice, also called the third person point of view). Be consistent in the voice that you use.
- Use parallel sentence structure.
- Introduce bullet points with a complete sentence (as was done above).
- Use numbers rather than bullets when steps must be completed in a certain order.

Of course, with the English language all rules are more like guidelines, and even the above items are open for some level of interpretation[8]. But they are good rules to follow in most professional and academic situations. Grammar is a subtle, but effective, way to show who you are. Clean up your grammar, spoken and written, and you change the way people see you. On the other hand, you do not want to over-speak, either. Do not try to impress people with language that is above their comprehension. Simple, clear language usually works best.

Remember also that English is a fluid language. Dictionaries are updated every year; new words are added, definitions to old words are modified, things change. For example, words like "office" are now being used not just as nouns, but as verbs; words like "gay" have moved from meaning festive, happy or bright to describing sexual orientation. It can be difficult to stay on top of these continuous changes, but it is important to be flexible in your interpretation of words, to understand that meanings do change, to attempt to use words appropriately and to occasionally use context to derive the meaning of words.

---

[8] As was mentioned in the "Introduction" to this text, the author herself sometimes bends and breaks these rules, when it suits the purpose of the text or you as the reader. For example, this text, in an effort to be easy to read and friendly, uses contractions, though such use may be frowned upon in an academic research paper or a professional progress report.

## Ethics in Communications

We have talked about credibility in writing, and how appearance can influence one's perceived credibility. But credibility can be more than perception; it can also be an ethical issue.

How we present ourselves and deal with situations can impact how we are perceived by others, and thus, how we are treated and what opportunities are open to us. In a business setting, ethical concerns can arise in many different contexts.

One common ethical concern in the modern business place surrounds surfing the Internet on company equipment and/or on company time. Consider the following scenario, listed in Figure 3.1.

---

Michael has been working in the IT department of Draco's Drafting and Design (DDD) for about a month. When he started he found it odd to learn that DDD did not have any type of content filtering in place to limit the web surfing of their employees. While he thought it was great that the company seemed to place much trust in their employees, he also felt that perhaps some level of filtering would be beneficial. This opinion was reinforced when, one day, Michael walked by a coworker's desk and saw him surfing a decidedly pornographic website. Michael mentioned this to his IT supervisor, who also was disturbed by the employee's surfing. After some discussion, Michael and the supervisor decided to take a look at the employee's hard drive after he left for the day. In doing so they found many photographs and videos that were seriously pornographic and, obviously, unsuitable for the professional workplace.

The next day Michael and the IT supervisor brought the issue to the attention of the senior department manager. They assumed that the manager would want to immediately enact some type of web filter. They were wrong. Instead, the manager was angry that Michael and the supervisor had violated the privacy of this employee by sneaking into his hard drive. The manager said that Michael and the supervisor should have contacted him or human resources about the problem and gone through proper channels. Michael was extremely surprised by this response and the reprimand that he received.

---

Figure 3.1: Scenario 1, Lenient Internet Policy

So, think about this scenario a moment. Then consider such questions as follow:
- Was Michael's original decision to tell his IT supervisor about the concern he observed the correct choice? If so, why? If not, why not?
- Were the actions of Michael and the supervisor appropriate?
- Was the response of the senior department manager appropriate?
- What might each participant in this scenario have done differently to cause a more positive outcome for all?

Another situation commonly faced in the business world is what to do when one suspects that others are misusing their authority or mishandling company resources, as presented in the following scenario of Figure 3.2.

Dana worked for a small company that supplied hardware and technical support for a local branch of the DNA consulting firm. One day Dana was at the DNA local office preparing an order to upgrade some of the computer systems. She was approached by John, an employee of DNA. John asked Dana to add two extra RAM modules to the hardware order for that month. When Dana asked why, John replied that his home computer was much too slow, and that he wanted to install some extra RAM in an effort to speed it up. Dana was surprised by this, and after a moments pause politely replied to John that she was not authorized to order parts other than those required to upgrade and repair the computers in the office. John became agitated and told Dana that no one cared, and she should just order the (insert four letter word here) RAM. Dana firmed her stance, and reiterated that she would not use company funds to purchase hardware for John's personal use, then left the room. As Dana thought about the situation, she remembered that this was not the first time that John had made requests that seemed to be for his benefit, not that of the company.

Later, Dana approached the supervisor of the DNA local office, and explained the incident, including her refusal. To her further surprise, the supervisor was not upset by John's request, but rather, was upset that Dana had not simply granted it quietly. Dana had an uneasy feeling that something was seriously amiss in this office.

Dana decided to draft a very professional letter to the head of the DNA corporate office, in which she detailed her various encounters with John, as well as the reaction of the supervisor. Dana later learned that an investigation had ensued, in which it was found that John and the supervisor had been working together to inappropriately benefit from and mishandle company funds, and that, in fact, other vendors had complained of similar encounters. Both John and the supervisor were fired.

Figure 3.2: Scenario 2 – Proper Use of Company Funds

So, again, think about this scenario for a moment, and what you might have done in a similar situation. Consider such questions as:

- Did Dana do the right thing in denying John's initial request, from an ethical perspective?
- Did Dana do the right thing in denying John's initial request, from a business perspective?
- Were Dana's decision to approach John's supervisor, and eventually to approach the head of the company good decisions, from both ethical and business perspectives?
- Had Dana made different decisions, might she have benefited professionally, perhaps through increased contracts with the local office?

As we consider these two scenarios, we realize that ethics and business do not always go hand-in-hand. In Scenario 1, Michael might have taken the moral high-ground in reporting his co-workers unethical web surfing. However, he may have also damaged his image with the office manager, which could hurt his career in indefinable ways. Similarly, while Dana's situation worked out well in Scenario 2, it could just as easily had been a disaster, and meant the loss of a major contract for her small company, if the head of the main office were also corrupt. These scenarios help us remember that behaving in an ethical way is not always easy, and does not always bring a happy ending. That is not to say that one should change their behavior, but rather to illustrate that ethics in the business world is a tangled web, and that each decision that we face on a day-to-day basis must be carefully considered.

Ethics are also very important in writing, professionally and academically. It is important that you are ethical in the information you convey, both in its accuracy and in giving credit where credit it due. Remember that when you write, for school, work or pleasure, it is important that you give proper credit to those whose work you borrow, whether you are rewording it or quoting.

*Using Source Material*

There is a joke among teachers that goes something like this: One college roommate was sitting at his computer working on a paper that was due the next day. The other roommate was waiting to leave for a big party and prompted the first to hurry up. The paper writer replied that he would be ready in a minute, he was almost done. The writer then continued to mumble under his breath, "select/copy/paste", "select/copy/paste", as he pulled information from Web sites and online books and pasted it, verbatim, into his paper. Satisfied, he saved the file, hit print, then ran off to the party.

Most of us realize that completely copying and pasting from Web sites or books is not a legitimate way to write any type of document. We also realize that it is wrong to have others do our work then take the credit, or to buy a term paper off the Internet. But even for those with the best of intentions, those who want to learn, the partial use of small bits of information without giving credit can seem acceptable. It's not.

Throughout life, we are called upon to write in many different forms. Often, specifically in academic and professional writing, we use reference material to learn from before writing, and to support the position that we are presenting. Using information gleaned from other sources is an excellent, and often necessary, way to add to the credibility of writing. However, it's[9] imperative that we always give proper credit to those that created the information that we use.

Citing references, particularly in academic writing, is not only ethical, but it is also an effective way to strengthen an argument. Most non-fiction books today rely heavily on information gathered from other sources. This is particularly true of science and technology books, where few of the ideas presented are completely original to the author. Using the work of others without acknowledging it, or receiving permission, when necessary, is plagiarism. In addition, there are various reasons why it is important to cite the sources that you use in a paper, as follow:

---

[9] Here the author seems to break her own rule, using a contraction. This is a matter of choosing to use casual language in an effort to reach the audience more readily.

- Citing sources, both through paraphrasing and directly quoting, illustrates that you have researched a topic and that your work is part of a larger body of literature on a subject.
- Citing sources creates a resource list for your reader, should they want to read in more depth on your topic.
- Proper citations give acknowledgement to the originator, giving credit where credit is due.
- Using source material illustrates that others support the ideas that you are setting forth, or helps you to balance your document by presenting alternative points of view.
- Citing resources properly ensures that you do not plagiarize.

We will discuss specifics on citing source material in a few pages.

## Plagiarism

According to Webster's Revised Unabridged Dictionary, to plagiarize is defined as, "To steal or purloin from the writings of another; to appropriate without due acknowledgement (the ideas or expressions of another)." Essentially, plagiarism is taking the words or ideas of another person, whether taken from their writing or their spoken word, and to use that information without giving proper credit to the originator.

### *Why Plagiarism is Wrong*

Plagiarism is wrong on many levels, both legally and morally. Plagiarism is essentially stealing and lying. Plagiarism not only cheats the person whose ideas were stolen, but it also cheats the author, who is not learning through their work; it cheats other students or coworkers who are doing their own work; and it cheats the business or University, who trusts the employee/student to do their own work.

### *Accidental and Intentional Plagiarism*

Not all plagiarism is malicious. Often, good people who did not set out with the intention to steal anyone's ideas accidentally plagiarize. Plagiarism is not always as clear as copying others work word for word or failing to give credit. Sometimes we change words slightly, or we do give credit to some extent, but the writing is still a form of plagiarism. This happens when we give credit in an improper or unclear way, or when we take too much information directly from a source, so much so that the work is not ours in any substantial way. Following are a few examples of plagiarism, intentional and accidental:

- using information, such as dates or other facts, without citing a source
- using a sentence or paragraph and changing only a few, unimportant words in an attempt to make it our own
- taking poor notes and losing track of what is our own idea and what was borrowed from source material
- using photos or other visual aids without crediting the source
- using photos or other visual aids to make money, even if the source is credited
- using another student's work and passing it off as your own. Note: This is unethical and considered plagiarism even if you have the other person's permission
- translating from a foreign language without rephrasing and citing references

- using papers that you wrote yourself without referencing them. Note: In most academic instances, you are expected to create original works. Thus, if you use information from a paper that you created, you must cite yourself as you would any other author[10]

*Avoiding Plagiarism*

Avoiding plagiarism is simple. Just give proper credit whenever you do the following with your writing:

- use someone else's ideas, opinions or words
- cite any specific facts or numbers
- use graphics or visuals created by someone else
- quote a person's direct words, written or spoken
- rephrase the words of another
- are uncertain of whether information should be cited or not

*Citing References*

A number of different style guides exist to help you properly cite source material. Among the most popular are the *Publication Manual of the American Psychological Association* (APA), the Modern Language Association (MLA) style, and the *Chicago Manual of Style*. Sometimes when you write, the style used to cite references (and format your paper) will be one of the guidelines you are given. Other times, choosing a proper citation method will be left up to you. Whatever method you choose, ensure that you supply the basic information. In most methods of citation it is important to provide the following information, in order to give proper credit:

- author/company/owner name
- book, article, paper or page/website name
- retrieval information, including web address, or publisher information

Above all, the documentation and formatting of references should be done in a way that reduces the effort of the reader, and makes it easy for them to locate a source that interests them.

It is also a good habit to provide a page number for direct quotations. Generally, you want to give a full citation in a reference list or bibliography at the end of your document. Then, within the document, whenever you use information (whether reworded or directly quoted word for word) you should use parenthesis or footnotes to identify basic information such as author and date – enough information that your reader, if interested, can locate the full citation in your reference list.

If you are interested in using a specific style manual, MLA, APA and *Chicago Manual of Style*, along with numerous other style guides, can be found at any bookstore.

---

[10] You might, at some point in this text, be wondering about the authors formatting of lists. Notice that sometimes lists items begin with a capitalized letter and end in a period. Other times they begin with a lower case letter and do not have a period at the end. When a list item is a grammatically complete sentence, it is formatted as a sentence, beginning with a capital letter and ending with a period. When a list item is a fragment, or incomplete sentence, it begins with a lower case letter and does not have a period at the end.

There are a few guidelines that apply to any writing, no matter what style guide you choose to follow. These include correct paraphrasing and the use of direct quotations.

### Paraphrasing

When you paraphrase, you take an idea that was presented by someone before you and use it in your own work, but you do so by rewording the idea substantially. Changing only a few unimportant words does not constitute proper rephrasing and is a form of plagiarism. Following are a few examples, good and bad.

Original Sentence:
"…writing is not a science. Rather, it is an art form, but an art form that can be learned. A good writer learns to balance words in a way that captures and maintains interest, while also communicating clearly, concisely and effectively."

Bad Paraphrase:
Writing is an art, not a science, and it can be learned. Good writing balances words, working to capture and hold the readers' interest and allow clear, concise and effective communications.

> Note: Far too much information is taken here; only a few unimportant words have been changed. It is still very recognizable as coming from the previous excerpt.

Good Paraphrase:
Good writing can be learned; with proper balance, a writer can communicate clearly and maintain reader interest.

> Note: This captures the most important ideas in the passage – not every idea, but those of most interest – and the writing varies considerably; this is barely recognizable, from a language perspective, as coming from the original source. Only the basic ideas remain.

### Using Direct Quotations

Direct quotations are a fine alternative to paraphrasing, especially in academic writing. But use quotations sparingly; quotes should only be used when the original excerpt is worded so well that to rephrase it would cause a loss of meaning. When you directly quote, remember the following guidelines:

- Surround the passage with quotation marks.
- Use an ellipsis (…) to indicate words that are left out.
- Use brackets [ ] to indicate words that were added for clarity in the quote.
- Do not alter the quote in any other way than those noted above.
- Always introduce quotes and weave them in to your own writing; do not just throw them in as complete sentences or paragraphs.
- Identify the author and page number for each quote.

*Common Knowledge vs. Referenced Information*

No all information needs to be cited. If you use ideas that you, yourself have developed or verified on your own, you do not need to cite it (unless it appeared in a previous work that you wrote). Even some facts are considered common knowledge and do not need to be cited. Such "common knowledge" information includes that which can be found in numerous places and is known by many people. Examples of common knowledge information are as follows:

- The Titanic sank on April 14, 1912.
- John F. Kennedy was assassinated in 1963.
- The major parts of a computer are a motherboard, central processing unit (CPU), RAM and hard drive.
- Many Americans have high speed, or broadband, Internet connections.

However, other, more specific information on the same topic may not be common knowledge and must be gathered from a reference. This information must be cited. Examples are as follows:

- On its maiden voyage, the Titanic had a lifeboat capacity of 1,178 people, barely enough for half of its passengers (Ballard, 1989).
- John Kennedy, Junior, turned three on November 25, 1963 – the day his father was buried (United Press, 1964).
- As of 1994, current popular PCs used 32-bit CPUs that handled 32-bit applications; however, 64-bit CPUs recently began coming to market that will also support older 32-bit applications (Mainelli, May 2004).
- As of 2002, there were more than 17 million broadband Internet users in the United States (Nua, 2003).

## Using Source Material for Research

At one time or another, most of us have tried to find information to provide a solution to a problem or to satisfy curiosity. During your academic or professional career, you have likely conducted research in order to create papers and answer questions. Research is a process that requires a strategy and flexibility – it is a planned, systematic approach designed to uncover all important aspects of a subject.

Research can be either primary or secondary. Primary research includes information you collect on your own through tools such as interviews, surveys, and experiments. More common is secondary research, which includes the gathering of information from books, journals, newspapers, videos and the like. The main challenge in conducting secondary research is evaluating the credibility, value and usefulness of available resources. Chapter 4 provides in-depth information on evaluating potential source-material.

## Summary

Credibility is important in many situations, but particularly when one is communicating with an audience, trying to sway them to a certain point of view or a certain way of thinking. Writing well, using good grammar and presenting attractive, well organized, easy-to-read papers are three ways of implicitly appearing credible. While grammar is one way that we show ourselves to be reliable sources of information, another way is to **be** reliable. Double-check your information. Verify, verify, verify. And when you are sure that your information is correct, present it in such a way that you instill confidence in the reader, that they believe you are correct because you sound like you are knowledgeable. When you use source material, be sure to give credit where credit is due. Citing references has a number of benefits, such as: giving proper credit to those whose ideas we borrow, showing additional support for a position you are writing about and helping your reader to find additional sources of information. Choosing credible sources to support your assertions is another way to ensure that your work is valuable to and respected by your audience.

**Additional Readings: Suggested Grammar Texts**

Gordon, K. E. (1993). The Deluxe Transitive Vampire: A Handbook of Grammar for the Innocent, the Eager and the Doomed. New York: Pantheon.

This book is the most fun you can have reading about grammar. For those interested in science fiction or the bizarre, this text is full of interesting, fun examples, using vampires, witches and gargoyles to illustrate effective English grammar. A great way to make a somewhat dry subject fun.

Pfeiffer, W. S. (2005). Pocket Guide to Technical Communication (4th Edition). Upper Saddle River, NJ: Prentice Hall.

This text provides basic grammar and punctuation and a number of tips for good writing. It also includes some excellent templates for various types of documents. This is a fantastic reference to keep on your desk.

Strunk, W., White, E.B., Angell, R. (1995). The Elements of Style, (4th Edition). Upper Saddle River, NJ: Longman.

This text is a classic in grammar, punctuation and basic writing style. It can be a bit dry, but overall is an excellent reference book and an easy read.

# CHAPTER 4

# Topic Selection and Research

---

*[A writer] may get the ideas he wishes to communicate directly from experience, he may get them indirectly through others, or he may, by recombining the elements of the actual experience, create this subject matter in his imagination.*
*~Earle*

# Chapter 4: Topic Selection and Research

## Introduction

There are different types of writers in the world, and certainly this text is not going to tell you what type you should be or what you can and cannot do. However, it will provide some solid suggestions that have served many writers well throughout history, particularly those who are less comfortable with writing, are writing on a topic that is not necessarily well understood or near and dear to them, or are writing within strict deadlines and/or requirements.

For some writers, words flow easily, and they prefer to simply write as a stream of consciousness, putting pen to paper and letting the ideas come forth and be recorded. A lucky few write so well in this fashion that they simply spell check and correct a few commas, and they are good to go. For most of us, though, the process works better if we make some plans first, brainstorm ideas, create an outline, then flesh the sections out. The following pages discuss this process. If you already have your own trusted and true method of writing, that's alright. But read on anyway – you may find a few nuggets of wisdom that will make your writing just that much easier. For those who do not have a specific writing method or find writing a less than enviable task, read on to have the process demystified and to learn a number of tricks that will make your next writing assignment a less stressful experience.

## Brainstorming and Choosing Topics

Sometimes you will be given an assignment that is specific, and your topic is already chosen for you. For example, perhaps you are the IT manager of a small architectural firm. The firm has decided to cut back their IT department. You are staying, along with a few help-desk people, but your boss wants to outsource hardware repair and continual network upgrading. She wants to hire a company to handle these aspects of IT, which will allow the company to cut its IT department by 25 percent. She has tasked you with researching local companies and presenting a report on the services and fees associated with potential outsource companies, along with your recommendation for which company is the best fit for your business needs. Your topic is chosen for you. You do not need to come up with a list of ideas about what to write on; you have been given something specific. You will still have a lot of work to do in order to get moving on the project and the report, but you have skipped one step that haunts many a writer – choosing a topic. Many are not able to skip this step, and choosing a topic, particularly in academic situations, can be as daunting a task as the actual writing.

Even fiction writers get hit with this issue. Authors look around their world, trying to decide what topics interest them and the public and what will make good stories. So to will be your job on many occasions, especially in academic writing. Perhaps you are taking a course in IT security to sharpen your skills, or you have decided to work toward an advanced degree and the course you are taking requires you to develop a research paper. Or maybe it is not school at all, perhaps you believe that have much to offer the field and want to write a magazine article on a topic in your area of expertise. But whether for school or personal achievement, you have to decide what topic to write about. So, you sit and you think. You brainstorm.

Brainstorming can be informal. It can be just you, sitting for a minute, where you could suddenly be struck by that *Eureka!* moment, the perfect inspiration just jumping into your lap. We should all be so lucky! For most of us, however, the "perfect" topic is ever elusive, and we struggle repeatedly with fleeting ideas and half-baked notions. But if we follow a solid process of more formal brainstorming, we can soon land upon a usable idea. Not every idea is a miraculous epiphany, but the brainstorming process can help you find an interesting, solid, writeable topic.

For effective brainstorming, start by sitting for a minute, in as quiet a place as your lifestyle will allow, pen and paper in hand (or, do it on the computer if you prefer). Think about the assignment you are tasked with[11]. Perhaps, "I want to write an article about IT security for publication in a computer magazine." Start out by writing "IT Security" at the top of your paper. Then, jot down every topic you can think of on the subject – everything. Don't make judgments about any of the potential ideas at this point, just write as many ideas as you can come up with. Some ideas, even those that seem poor, may lead to other ideas as you go. For example, you might begin like that shown in Figure 4.1:

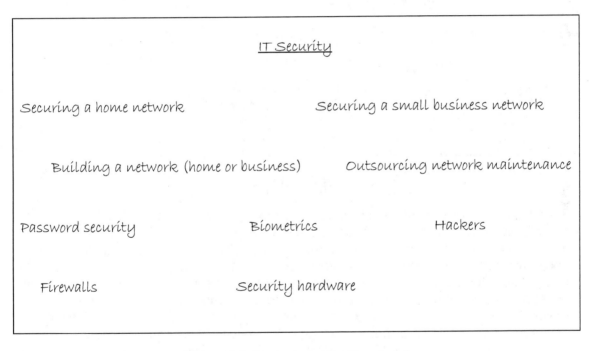

Figure 4.1: Brainstorming, Session 1

Once you have listed every topic that you can think of in the area of IT security, look over the list and begin to consider the ideas on a basic level. Read the list and see if any of the ideas spark other ideas or can be sub-divided into smaller topics that might also

---

[11] Notice that this sentence ends with a preposition. You have probably been told throughout your writing life not to end sentences with a preposition. This is a gray area in English grammar. Many people will tell you that it is against the laws of English grammar to end sentences this way. However, the authors experience (and research) shows that there is no such "law", rather, it is a guideline that many English writers and academics follow, but which others do not. This sentence, for example, could be written, "Think about the assignment with which you are tasked." This does not end in a preposition, but it does not "sound" right, it does not read as most of us speak. Thus, as with many other guidelines in this book, the author encourages you to follow this rule, or not, as seems appropriate to your own writing.

work. Cross off any subjects you do not like or which do not seem to fit what you are looking for. You may, at this point, even decide on a focus; for example, home networking or small business. Now, add your thoughts to your brainstorming notes, perhaps something as shown in Figure 4.2:

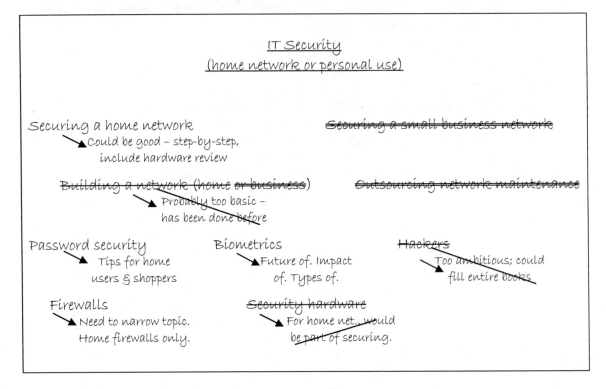

Figure 4.2: Brainstorming, Session 2

Now you have crossed out the topics that you know you do not want to tackle, specifically, business networks. Then you made some brief notes on each remaining topic – ideas for direction or reasons to exclude them. You then crossed off those that, upon further reflection, you decided to exclude for whatever reason. You are left with four possible topics: securing a home network, password security, biometrics, and home network firewalls. That's some good progress; from a world of possibilities and absolutely no direction you have come up with four interesting, potentially usable topics, in just minutes. But you only need one topic, so you need to continue the process.

By this point, perhaps one topic has jumped out at you. The more you think about it, the more you realize that your neighborhood newspaper might like to run an article on securing home networks in their technology section; you think you can sell that piece. Great! You've settled on a topic and can move on. But, you might not have a topic jumping out in your mind yet. At this point, all four topics seem just as good as the others. Let's go deeper. Reorganize and rewrite your ideas, omitting everything that has been crossed out, adding further notes you can think of, and crossing out any that you decide against, something like that shown in Figure 4.3, on the following page.

---

Home Network Security

Securing a home network:
    * step by step instructions
    * hardware review
NOTES: this might not stand alone,
may need to come after an article on
setting up a network – too large a scope.

Biometrics:
    * Future of
    * Impact of
    * Types of
NOTES: interesting topic
could be brief overview.
would lend itself to many
fun graphics.

Password security:
    * Tips for home users
    * Tips for shopping safety
NOTES: interesting topic, and
Valuable to people.

Home network firewalls:
    * Hardware vs. software
    * Setting up
    * Maintaining
    *Disadvantages
NOTE: lot of good info
and potential directions,
but seems too big for
short article.

---

Figure 4.3: Brainstorming, Selection Process

In just a short amount of time, you have made great progress in narrowing this topic. You are down to two ideas: biometrics and password security. So, let's take one more crack at narrowing it to just one. The next step might be to consider how much personal knowledge you have of the topic you have chosen and what resources will be available to you when researching the topic. You can begin by jotting down your evaluation of your own knowledge. Then do a brief online search of the topics and see if there are many sources you will be able to draw upon. If you are writing a research paper, ensuring that you will have access to ample source material will be a high priority. After your few minutes of Internet searching, you might have the following notes, as shown in Figure 4.4.

<u>Home Network Security</u>

Biometrics:
* Future of
* Impact of
* Types of
NOTES: interesting topic could be brief overview.
Would lend itself to many fun graphics.
KNOWLEDGE: I know a bit about this topic, a solid background,
but would also like to learn more myself.
RESOURCES: There are many, many sites and texts about biometrics. Many
are very technical, but there is ample material to draw from to develop an
interesting, concise article giving people general information about what they
might start seeing – and experiencing – in the near future. I'm liking this
topic a lot!

Password security
* Tips for home users
* Tips for shopping safety
NOTES: interesting topic, and valuable to people.
KNOWLEDGE: I know little about this topic, really. But it is interesting.
RESOURCES: In my quick search I found a number of sources, but most
seemed aimed at businesses and how to require employees to choose difficult-to
-guess passwords. It could be hard to find a lot of information that would be
valuable to the average home user.

Figure 4.4: Brainstorming, Narrowed Down to Two

From the above notes, the topic choice seems clear – biometrics it is! As a bonus, you already have a brief start on your next step, the outline. You have a few bullet points to begin with, and hopefully you have already had the foresight to bookmark the biometric Web sites that you visited. Of course, you should always be well organized and thus should have already created a folder in your favorites or bookmarks titled biometrics, so you can gather all of your links there as you work on the article. Now, with topic in hand, you move on to the outline.

**Outlines**

Outlines serve many purposes. They help us to get started, turning what can be a daunting, blank page into a shell, ready to hold the wonderful keystrokes that stream from our fingertips. They help us to organize our thoughts, to begin a document in an organized fashion, which limits the revisions that you have to do later. Outlines, if you take some liberties, can also be great ways to house notes and guidelines you do not want to forget as you write.

When developing an outline, some people prefer pen and paper. Others, such as the author[12], prefer to start a computer file that can be continually updated. Either is fine, though in this section, we will assume you are on a computer. Those of you who prefer the feel of pen in hand can easily modify what is written here and jump on the keyboarding bandwagon at whatever stage seems appropriate to you.

Begin your outline simply. Open a new file and put a working title at the top. It can be a basic title, even just the subject. You can work on an actual title later, whenever the inspiration hits you. Next, put in the few bullet points you already have, along with, of course, an introduction (which you can title "Introduction," or something more descriptive – the choice is yours). Note that if you use MS Word as your word processor, you can choose the "outline view" under the "view" menu to help you create your initial outline. Later, you can change to normal or print view as you begin to flesh out your actual paper. For your biometrics topic, you might start with an outline as shown in Figure 4.5.

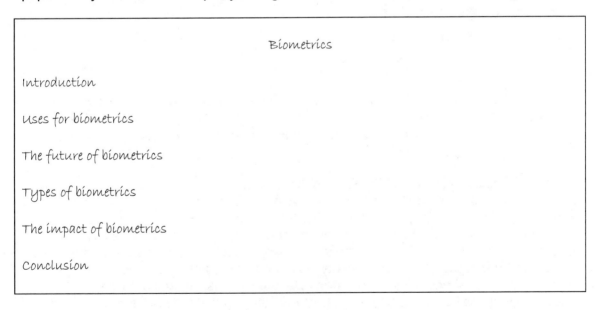

Figure 4.5: Outline

Well done, in 30 minutes or so you went from no topic at all to a solid, if brief, outline of a single topic. Excellent. Now, let's take a minute and look at your outline. At a glance you see that "Introduction" is a boring start to such an interesting topic. So, let's change that to something better….. maybe "Defining Biometrics". You could use, "What are

---

[12] You may feel that this reference to the author is very casual, and somewhat unusual for a text book. Actually, it is a style used often in research texts, where the author needs to refer to their own experience, and was used here because the authors experience seemed relevant to you, the reader.

Biometrics?" But since none of your other headings will likely be in interrogative form, this would not be parallel. It is better to have all headings be statements, not questions. Next you see that "Types of Biometrics" should probably come before uses and the future – you should tell "what" before why or how. And speaking of future, if you are going to discuss that, you should probably discuss the past first. After a few more minutes of tweaking, you end up with a new outline as shown in Figure 4.6.

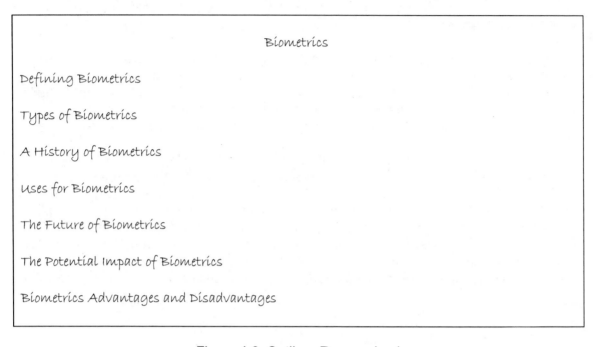

Figure 4.6: Outline, Reorganized

Now that is a solid outline! You can continue to flesh it out as you go along; certainly outlines can and do change as you write, and that's just fine. But this is a good starting point. You no longer have that scary blank page staring at you, and you have solid direction for moving on.

For the fastidious writer who has guidelines to write within, a specific audience to meet, and purpose to accomplish, there is one final step. This step, which was touched upon in Chapter 1, is to add in notes that delineate the specifics of audience, purpose, and guidelines, notes that will be useful to you, as you write. For example, let's say now that your biometrics topic is not going to be a magazine article, but rather a term paper for a course you are taking in network security. You have been given an audience, purpose, and a number of criteria to meet. You don't want to risk missing any of these or forgetting them as you write, or your grade may suffer. So, you add a few notes to the outline, notes that will be deleted later, after each note has been accomplished. For example, after carefully reading your assignment sheet, you might add to your outline, as shown in Figure 4.7.

---

Biometrics

AUDIENCE: Instructor (with advanced IT knowledge) and classmates (with varied experience)
PURPOSE: To write a research paper that accomplishes the following: shows an
    understanding of one topic in IT, showcases good writing skills, uses source material
    effectively.

NOTES: Must use at least five sources to support position.
    Must use APA format.
    Must be 10 pages in length.
    Due by March 31st.
    Every spelling error causes a loss of 5 points (spell-check!!).
    Must have table of contents and abstract.

Defining Biometrics

Types of Biometrics

A History of Biometrics

Uses for Biometrics

The Future of Biometrics

The Potential Impact of Biometrics

A Summary of Biometrics Advantages and Disadvantages

---

Figure 4.7: Outline, with Requirements

Now, you are ready to start your research and note taking.

## Beginning the Actual Research

Since the beginning of time, man has recorded his knowledge and history in writing. From cave writings, to clay tablets, to the earliest recordings on bamboo, silk, and papyrus, man has written down information and stored it for future generations. Libraries began appearing thousands of years before what we consider modern times, and ancient texts were hand copied and archived long before the advent of the printing press. Over the millennia, man has progressed not only in his amount of knowledge, but also in his recording and storage of that knowledge. We now live in a time when new concepts in information technology are continually being developed and information is easier and less expensive to find, store, and retrieve than ever before. Even people in the 1970s and 1980s had no idea how easy information would soon become to store and to transmit and how quickly we would progress into not just an information age, but an information bonanza.

In the past, academic research involved the physical act of sifting through mountains of printed matter, looking for pertinent information. Researchers and scholars hunted through card catalogs in attempts to identify sources, then marched up and down the library aisles, looking through Dewey decimals, hunting for the printed material. This was before the dawn of the computer age. In recent decades, online public access catalogs have almost completely replaced traditional card catalogs. These databases are more than just computerized version of ancient card catalogs; they provide in-depth information about the sources they house, often even holding complete articles and texts. Researchers can now locate information with just a few keystrokes, and often they can not only identify information through online databases, but actually retrieve information stored in databases, as opposed to looking in printed books or journals.

Ironically, many books have been published to help students learn to use online research tools. Some such texts from the mid 1990s offer step-by-step guidelines for finding information in computer databases. They also offer advice on using computers as a writing tool. Some of these same texts caution writers to avoid using the formatting features of their word processor, implying that to do so causes a loss of integrity when moving files from system to system or over the Internet. However, this is an outdated attitude, as word processing software is now highly compatible from system to system, and software such as Adobe Acrobat allows the conversion of files to a format that is portable from computer to computer, system to system, with complete file integrity. By printing books about how to research using computers, the industry actually illustrates how quickly the printed word can become out of date and how valuable more recent online sources can be. Such online research is increasing in popularity among academic and commercial researchers.

### Types of Research

There are three basic types of research: primary, secondary, and tertiary research. Primary sources include those that contain raw data, including surveys, experiment data, and public records. Secondary sources include those where the information has been processed in some way, including journal articles, books, and some Web sites. Tertiary sources includes those that compile information, such as encyclopedias, dictionaries, other reference books, and databases. The Internet can be a valuable tool for collecting all of these types of information, but it can be particularly useful for writing academic and professional papers using secondary and tertiary sources.

In 1952 one researcher wrote, "Science by its very nature is a structure which grows by the addition of new material on top of a giant edifice formed by earlier workers" (Wilson, p.10). No matter what field one is in, research will be needed at some point. The World Wide Web can be a tremendous asset in such pursuits.

### Current Technology

Computer databases have revolutionized information storage and retrieval. But there may still be information that is not retrievable online. It is important to remember that the method of research must change to suit the particularly project, not vice versa. But for business and IT professionals, most research can be completed through the Internet or computer libraries.

There are numerous advantages to properly executed online data storage and retrieval. The main advantage is space; computers allow for the storage of mass quantities of information in small amounts of space. Multiple volumes of journals, encyclopedias, and more can be stored in single databases or CD-ROMs with amazing search capabilities. Computer indexes take up far less space than printed card catalogs, and allow for the inclusion of more detailed abstracts. Electronic data can also be accessed more easily, printed, downloaded, e-mailed – all without the expense of paper and ink, the destruction of trees, or the work of hand-written notes. Electronic databases can be easily searched using keywords and other tools, and can be searched much more quickly than traditional card catalogs.

The Web and online databases have the ability to provide researchers with amazing amounts of information, quickly. But, electronic sources present disadvantages as well. Information on the Internet can be disorganized and difficult to find. The content runs the gamut, from grade-school book reports to doctoral dissertations, to works by award-winning authors. There is often no rhyme or reason to the content or organization, and no librarian to pull it all together. Web sites are sometimes available one day, gone the next. Access can be limited, and graphics and multi-media information can take a long time to load, especially during peak hours. Response times from servers can be slow, and sites can be replete with advertisements and unwanted information. Time can also be a negative in some aspects of Internet research.

In one way, time is perhaps the greatest advantage the Internet has over traditional library research. The Internet is like a library that never closes. It transcends space and time, allowing one to research at any time of the day or night. But, even with the Internet, time can be a limitation. For example, while electronic encyclopedias can be full of information, easy to navigate and easy to update, they still are never completely up to date, requiring months, at best, to research and update new ideas. Time can also be a downfall, in that information does not stay on the Internet forever. As was mentioned above, sometimes, a page that is there one day, is gone the next, and information found can be difficult or impossible to find again. To combat this, it is important to cite URL addresses in your reference page, but another good idea is to make a back-up copy of important information you find online. This can be done electronically by saving copies of files you find, or by "printing" any screen to a graphics program or a processor such as Adobe Acrobat (as long as you are not infringing on copyright or distributing the source on your own). In this way, you can archive important information you find for future reference, should it become unavailable online.

### Using Online Sources Effectively

The Internet can offer an amazing road into a wilderness of information and data. But the wise researcher keeps in mind that this wilderness is untamed, and thus everything found must be evaluated and questioned, not taken as unconditional truth. Cyberspace is replete with bad information and even intentional misinformation. To wade through this much information, it is important to begin with a plan of attack. Likely your desire for information will lead you to search engines such as Google.com, Yahoo.com or Ask.com. It is important that you read any tips and tricks provided by these sources so that you understand the most effective way to conduct your search through their site. One basic idea is to begin your search in an encyclopedia or other reference source, to gain a foundational understanding of the topic to be researched and to help identify keywords and related ideas that can be used in more extensive searching later. Think of every possible permutation of keywords in your topic. Remember that a search for "history of lunch box" may provide distinctly different results than "history of lunchbox." It is imperative to think of variations and search thoroughly. Then, as a researcher, you must learn not just to locate information, but to evaluate its credibility and appropriateness.

Research is not simply about finding information, but also about determining what information will be useful. Evaluating resources, especially online sources, is an ongoing process where the researcher looks at the source and determines its authority, the quality of content, the accuracy, and the currency. No one Web source, unless infinitely reliable, should be used in a vacuum, without support from outside sources.

Determining the credibility of Web information is a critical step in using online sources effectively. There are various types of online sources. There are search engines (such as Google.com and Yahoo.com) that help one to find information. There are online databases such as Academic Search Premier by EBSCOHOST and googlescholar. There are informational sites, commercial sites (which end in .com), non-profit sites (which end in .org), educational sites (which end in .edu), governmental sites (which end in .gov), and more. Two pieces of important information which help determine a site's credibility are the type of site and the owner of the site. One way to find out who owns a site is to check out the "About us" page, found on many sites.

Commercial Web sites are sometimes no more than advertising or hyperbole in disguise. But such sites can often have excellent information available for free – you simply need to approach such information with caution. It is important to verify information from such sources and to check the accuracy of the information against a second or third source. Consider the source, the Internet address, the author or owner, when the site was last updated, the presence of commercial support, and the accuracy of information. Other smart steps include verifying the information with a second or third source, considering credibility based upon presentation, looking for obvious bias, and considering whether the information provided is primary or secondary.

To illustrate the potential for misinformation on the Internet, consider the following. In April 2007, a search was conducted on Google.com, using the search term "Titanic". The search produced more than 120 million results. At a glance, most seemed to directly refer to the R.M.S. Titanic, which sunk tragically in 1912. But if, when conducting the search, Titanic is misspelled and the term "Titanc" is searched, more than 9,000 results are returned. At a glance, at least those on the first few pages are indeed referring the wreck of 1912. Of course, one is left to wonder how reliable a source is when it misspells such a simple, important keyword. But by contrast, when "Titanic" was searched on the academic database "EBSCOHOST," more than 10,000 results were returned, and a search on the misspelled "Titanc" returns just one result, which was in a non-English language and apparently had nothing to do with the sinking of the oceanic liner. This illustration simply shows that a researcher is more likely to find erroneous information on the free, public Web than in a scholarly database, and thus such Web-based sources should come under significant scrutiny.

*Previewing*

When you are attempting to choose a credible source, begin by previewing selected sources. This includes scanning the source, reading tables of contents in a book, looking at the menu or site map of a Web page, and so forth. Generally, you can make a basic assumption about the potential usefulness and credibility of a source at a glance – first impressions can mean a lot. Next, begin to read the sources you deem worthy of detailed attention. Eliminate data that seems biased, is too out of date for your topic, or appears to be from tertiary or suspect sources.

When evaluating Internet sites, remember that access to the Internet is not limited or regulated — anyone can post anything that they want, whether it is accurate or not. The accuracy of information found on commercial sites is sometimes in question, but university and government Web sites are usually highly credible. After you determine that a source seems credible, extract as much useful information into organized notes as needed. Remember to cite the source of the research each time you pull data or a quote. Evaluate your choice of research items according to the guidelines below.

When evaluating books, articles, or Web sites for credibility, ensure the following:

- The document is credibly written, grammatically correct, well organized, and gives an appearance of credibility.
- The author of the document has the experience to write on this topic.
- If reviewing a paper online, the research question chosen for the paper was succinct, clear, and readily supported by research material.
- The scope of the topic chosen was sufficiently narrow to research it thoroughly.
- The materials referenced in the body of the paper or Web site were accurately cited.
- The bibliography demonstrates that the resources chosen were most pertinent to the research question (rather than listing everything available on the topic).
- The bibliography included a variety of resources (scholarly journals, popular journals, Internet resources, technical reports, personal interviews, and newspaper sources).
- The materials used in the bibliography were both historical and current (if relevant) and presented in a standard style format.
- Sources used are fair, objective, lack hidden motivation, and illustrate quality control of content.
- Any sources used in the document were reliable in that each writer did the following:
    - distinguished between fact and fiction
    - differentiated between relevant and irrelevant information
    - identified the author's purpose and point of view accurately
    - identified unsubstantiated statements
    - identified inconsistencies, errors, and omissions
    - identified bias, stereotyping, and incorrect assumptions
    - was able to compare and contrast different points of view properly
    - included author's original ideas, properly cited

*Pulling It Together*

Positive and negative, enough information and too much information, good and bad, the Internet has it all. But the Internet also opens up a very interesting possibility for the academic and professional researcher, and for instructors – plagiarism. The Internet allows access to amazing amounts of information from a prolific number of sources around the world. Such technology can make it easy, even tempting, for scholars and practitioners to  steal information, whether knowingly or inadvertently. The Internet allows for the taking of entire documents, or plagiarism through the copy/paste of words, phrases, or paragraphs. Plagiarism is often born not just of laziness, but of carelessness, ignorance, and opportunity.  But the diligent researcher is careful to give credit where credit is due, as is discussed in Chapter 3.

Computers and online sources can help collect data, gather information, increase knowledge and understanding, and aid in communication, but it is important to remember that they are not the only means to these ends. To ensure that your research is well rounded, the World Wide Web is best used in conjunction with traditional research. One can use the Web to search a card catalog in a local library before ever leaving home, making time spent at the library more efficient while still allowing for the use of actual printed material, achieving some level of balance between texts, journals, and Web sites.

The Web is much more than the garbage, entertainment, bigotry, and pornography it is sometimes perceived as; it is a virtual library, available anywhere at any time to any one, a library full of pictures and audio/video files, articles, books, names, addresses, and much more. It is not appropriate to use the Internet for all research, but rather such technology should be applied carefully, and in conjunction with other research types and other support.  One needs simply to exercise some caution and common sense in determining when the Internet is the best choice for information retrieval, and to identify the most credible sources of that information. With a little work, the Internet can provide a plethora of valuable information for almost anyone researching within any field.

**Taking Notes**

Once you have identified some solid sources, you will want to begin reviewing them and taking notes. When you think about taking notes, you may picture grade school with visions of note cards dancing in your head. That was a great, old-school method of note organization, and one that many people still use today. But, in the information age, electronic note-taking can be more efficient. If you are a fan of note cards, by all means, continue. But consider the suggestions in this section as well.

At this point in the writing process, you should have a brief outline with a few notes as we went over earlier. You may want to do a "save as" on your outline file and create a "notes" or "research" file. That way, you can leave your original file for when you begin the actual writing of your paper, but still have a copy of your outline and notes handy as a skeleton to house your notes. To begin with, you might populate the various sections of your outlines with bits of information that you know based on personal experience. Everything you can think of, throw it in as brief phrases, no complete sentences yet; save that for later. This process could take some time, and it does not have to be done all at once. As ideas come to you, your own, original ideas, you can add them in as appropriate.

The next step is likely where most of your content will come from, especially if you are developing a research paper. This is the use of source material. As was discussed in Chapter 3, this is a serious responsibility. The first step in using source material effectively is to judge the credibility of the source. The second step is to take meticulous notes, ensuring that you clearly delineate what thoughts are not yours but rather come from a source, what source they come from, and, if a direct quote, properly quoting it and ensuring that you copy the quote into your notes accurately.

There are a few ways for taking notes on sources you have located. Some writers might read the article and just make a few notes on paper. That's okay, but there are more effective ways to use articles and Web sites, especially if you are earning a degree or work in a field where you might have to revisit the topic you are writing on in the future and thus wish to collect sources on the topic for future reference. In these cases you will likely want to carefully track and maintain all of the articles you read. You can begin by book-marking any Web sites and keeping your files organized[13]. But you can take this a step further by using an Adobe .pdf creator or other similar software to save a copy of an article or Web site you are reviewing. Then, either print the article in hard copy and make your notes by hand, or save a tree and your file cabinet space and save a computer copy and make your notes on that. Again, Adobe Acrobat is an excellent tool for doing this. As of this printing, you can purchase a copy for under $200, and if you are a student, you can probably get a copy for just under $100. There are also some free .pdf creators on the Web and other similar methods of archiving pages and articles. Adobe allows you to save Web pages and articles, then use mark-up tools to make comments, high-light important points, underline – nearly everything you could do with pen and paper. It is an exceptional way to keep notes that are easy to file and come back to in the future.

On the following pages is an excerpt from a Web site about conducting research using the deep Web. This is actually a three-page listing: the first page shows a copy of the Overview page of the site, as converted to Adobe Acrobat. The next page shows the same excerpt, but with comments added in, as if the article were being reviewed for use as a source in a research paper on using the Effective Internet Search Strategies. The third page shows the APA citation of the Web site, along with a brief annotation – this is often called an annotated bibliography or annotated list of references. Creating brief listings like this is an excellent way to track the various sources you read throughout your career or education. You can look back to see if there was information you could use without having to completely reread every article that you have saved. See Figures 4.8, 4.9 and 4.10, on the following pages, for the excerpt.

---

[13] You may have noticed that in a few places, information (such as this comment on bookmarking websites) is repeated. As a technical or business writer, you may find this unnecessarily redundant, and wonder if such writing should not be more concise. Generally, you would be correct – technical and professional writing should be concise, and avoid repetition. However, this is a text book, designed to teach you, and reading something twice is more effective than reading it once, thus you may sometimes find information redundant. As always, it is a matter of violating apparent rules to properly address the text's audience and purpose.

# Overview

## *Introduction*

The Internet links computer networks and people across our planet. This USA author received a booklet of postcards with beautiful photos of Moscow from a programmer in Russia that he "met" online while troubleshooting an application. Several years ago the author's wife's daughter and her husband went on an African safari by invitation as the guests of Africans they met online. Twenty years ago, events like this did not happen to ordinary people, today they are commonplace thanks to the global reach of the Internet. The Internet allows us to share files, information and relationships.

This guide is meant to aid IT researchers in finding higher quality information in less time. In a simplified description, the Web consists of these two parts – the surface Web and the deep Web (invisible Web or hidden Web). The deep Web came into public awareness only recently with the publication of the landmark book by Sherman & Price (2001), "The Invisible Web: Uncovering Information Sources Search Engines Can't See." Since then, many books, papers and websites have emerged to help the searcher further explore this vast landscape. Why the fuss? Don't search engines and directories do everything needed by a researcher? Let's explore this further. Search engines and directories provide great services, but they are limited. Search engines, index less than 1% of the Web (BrightPlanet, 2005, Deep Web FAQ). The remaining 99% of the Web is located in the deep Web. In addition, information in the deep Web is of higher quality, that is, less "noise" and more focused. If you are searching for information using only surface Web search engines, you are missing 99% of the content of the Web. Moreover, 95% of the deep Web is free publicly accessible information (Deep Web FAQ).

Today's search engines are marvelous research tools; however, searches often yield more trash than treasure. Sifting through the junk to find the gems can consume large amounts of time. It is noteworthy that the majority of users are frustrated by search engines, Chamy (2000, para. 2) has found that "Web-rage is uncaged after twelve minutes of fruitless searching." A typical keyword search may uncover millions of "hits." Even fine tuning, by tweaking your keywords and using the advanced search features of search engines, can yield results that are less than desirable. More importantly, however, is the vast amount of information missed by search engines. It is in these situations where the deep Web can be of help. The deep Web is not a substitute for surface search engines, but a complement to a complete search approach.

The imagery used for the Web is a spider's web that covers the planet. Search engines are the spiders that crawl all over the Web to extract and index text from websites. Hence, these search engines are called spiders or crawlers. Surface search engines crawl from static web page to static web page to extract text from HTML then index these words. Information stored in databases is not in a format these search engines can access. Databases are accessed dynamically by queries using the retrieval tools unique to the database. An analogy would be that surface search engines can see all the birds floating on the ocean, but can not see the fish. You need sonar to look through the depths of the water to see the fish and a fishing pole or net to catch the fish.

Figure 4.8: TechDeepWeb Overview Page (Gruchawka, 2006)

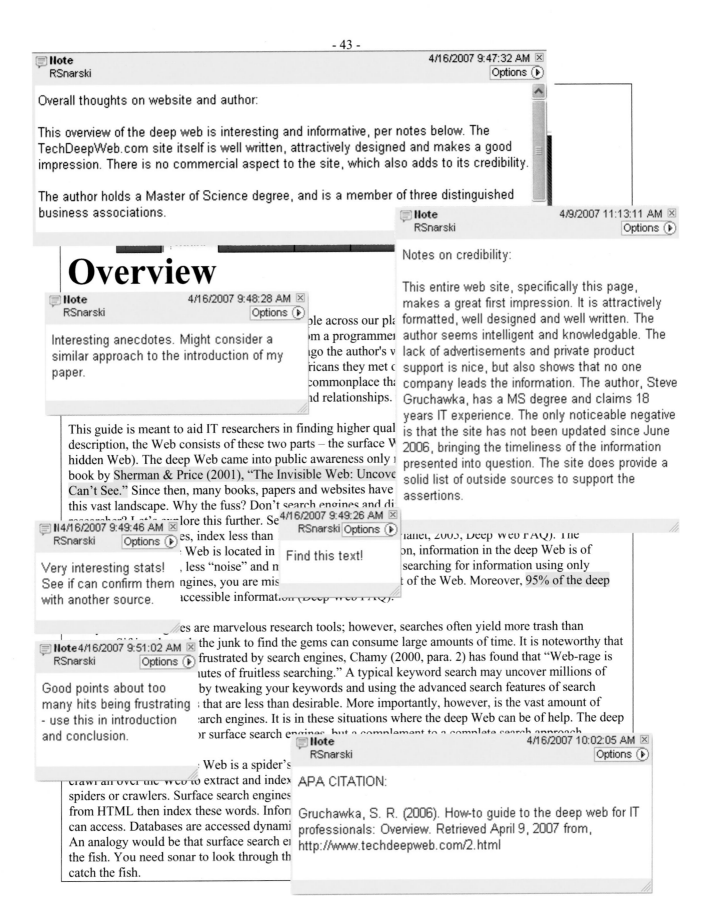

**Note**    RSnarski     4/16/2007 9:47:32 AM ⊠   Options ⊙

Overall thoughts on website and author:

This overview of the deep web is interesting and informative, per notes below. The TechDeepWeb.com site itself is well written, attractively designed and makes a good impression. There is no commercial aspect to the site, which also adds to its credibility.

The author holds a Master of Science degree, and is a member of three distinguished business associations.

# Overview

**Note**    RSnarski     4/16/2007 9:48:28 AM ⊠   Options ⊙

Interesting anecdotes. Might consider a similar approach to the introduction of my paper.

**Note**    RSnarski     4/9/2007 11:13:11 AM ⊠   Options ⊙

Notes on credibility:

This entire web site, specifically this page, makes a great first impression. It is attractively formatted, well designed and well written. The author seems intelligent and knowledgable. The lack of advertisements and private product support is nice, but also shows that no one company leads the information. The author, Steve Gruchawka, has a MS degree and claims 18 years IT experience. The only noticeable negative is that the site has not been updated since June 2006, bringing the timeliness of the information presented into question. The site does provide a solid list of outside sources to support the assertions.

This guide is meant to aid IT researchers in finding higher qual... description, the Web consists of these two parts – the surface W... hidden Web). The deep Web came into public awareness only... book by Sherman & Price (2001), "The Invisible Web: Uncove... Can't See." Since then, many books, papers and websites have... this vast landscape. Why the fuss? Don't search engines and di...

**Note**    RSnarski     4/16/2007 9:49:46 AM ⊠   Options ⊙

Very interesting stats! See if can confirm them with another source.

**Note**    RSnarski   4/16/2007 9:49:26 AM ⊠   Options ⊙

Find this text!

...lanet, 2003, Deep Web FAQ). The ...on, information in the deep Web is of ...searching for information using only ...t of the Web. Moreover, 95% of the deep

...es are marvelous research tools; however, searches often yield more trash than ...the junk to find the gems can consume large amounts of time. It is noteworthy that ...frustrated by search engines, Chamy (2000, para. 2) has found that "Web-rage is ...utes of fruitless searching." A typical keyword search may uncover millions of ...by tweaking your keywords and using the advanced search features of search ...that are less than desirable. More importantly, however, is the vast amount of ...arch engines. It is in these situations where the deep Web can be of help. The deep ...or surface search engines, but a complement to a complete search approach.

**Note**    RSnarski     4/16/2007 9:51:02 AM ⊠   Options ⊙

Good points about too many hits being frustrating - use this in introduction and conclusion.

...Web is a spider's ...crawl all over the Web to extract and index ...spiders or crawlers. Surface search engines ...from HTML then index these words. Infor... can access. Databases are accessed dynami... An analogy would be that surface search e... the fish. You need sonar to look through th... catch the fish.

**Note**    RSnarski     4/16/2007 10:02:05 AM ⊠   Options ⊙

APA CITATION:

Gruchawka, S. R. (2006). How-to guide to the deep web for IT professionals: Overview. Retrieved April 9, 2007 from, http://www.techdeepweb.com/2.html

Figure 4.9: TechDeepWeb Overview Page (with notes)

Annotated Bibliography on Internet Research Strategies

Gruchawka, S. R. (2006). How-to guide to the deep web for IT professionals: Overview. Retrieved April 9, 2007 from, http://www.techdeepweb.com/2.html

This website provides a basic overview of the "deep web", an area of the web that includes "99%" of the Internet's actual content (para. 2). The site discusses strategies for searching this deep web, rather than just the 1% that most inexperienced searchers find. The author and site appear very credible. Though it had not been updated in some time, and the resources list was incomplete. This would be a good site to check back on in the future, particularly to see if more resources have been added.

Figure 4.10: Annotated Bibliography of TechDeepWeb Site

Reading articles and Web sites should be an active experience. Many of us have been taught to highlight some key words or sentences here and there while reading. But if you highlight everything of interest in an article, all you end up with is a very yellow article. When you want to use the information, you have to read it again and think, again, why you highlighted what you did, and consider, again, how that information is pertinent to what you are doing. However, if you take more active notes, as the above sample shows, you save yourself much work in the future. You can read, at a glance, what you thought was interesting or noteworthy about each section you marked. You can see, at a glance, where you might use this information or what information you may want to revisit in the future. Look again at the previous sample. Think about how much less effective it would be if paragraphs and sentences were just highlighted with no notes.

When you conduct research, a good practice is to gather a large number of sources and review them per the previous example. Then, begin taking your notes on separate paper, transferring the most important information from the articles into your notes. At this point, it is important to keep **very careful track** of where the ideas and notes come from, identify what is a direct quote, and note anything that is your own idea.

Let's take just a moment to look at an example of how your notes might look. Say that you are still working on that biometrics paper. You have so far evaluated three sources: an article by an author named Smith, a book by Byerson, and a Web site owned by TechyCorp. You might have some notes that look something like the example in Figure 4.11.

Biometrics

AUDIENCE: Instructor (with advanced IT knowledge) and classmates (with varied experience)

PURPOSE: To write a research paper that accomplishes the following: shows an understanding of one topic in IT, showcases good writing skills, uses source material effectively.

NOTES: Must use at least five sources to support position. Must use APA format. Must be 10 pages in length. Due by March 31st. Every spelling error causes a loss of 5 points (spell-check!). Must have table of contents and abstract.

Defining Biometrics

TechyWeb defines biometrics as, "The use of physical human traits, such as fingerprints, retinal scans or voice recognition, to identify individuals that are allowed access to a specific electronic system" (from www.techyweb.com, April 8, 3rd paragraph).

My idea: Find other definitions and see if there are any contradictions to be explored.

Types of Biometrics

Fingerprints (Techyweb & Byerson), Retinal scans (Techyweb & Byerson), voice recognition (Techyweb & Byerson). Palm print recognition (Smith).

My note: what about DNA? Is that a potential future biometric? Look into that.

A History of Biometrics

Little info in Techyweb, Byerson, or Smith. Look for other sources.

Uses for Biometrics

Security computer systems at work and home (Smith article).

"Biometrics are of paramount importance in the defense industry" (Byerson, p.5).

The Future of Biometrics

My idea: The future of biometrics is still uncertain, as various ramifications and situations need to be considered. For example, fingerprints seem like a great biometric protection; however, we have all seen numerous movies where a villain simply cuts off the hand of the person whose print they need, and uses that to access a fingerprint protected system. Is this a real scenario to be considered before biometrics are implemented?

The Potential Impact of Biometrics

A Summary of Biometrics Advantages and Disadvantages

Figure 4.11: Outline, with Notes

Notice that in the above notes, every idea clearly has the author listed who originated the idea. Direct quotes are clearly quoted, with page numbers given. In fact, when taking your notes, it is a good idea to list page numbers even for things that are not direct quotes, in case you want to read more about that idea later if you need to flesh out the section or decide to change your scope a bit.

In Chapter 3 we discussed ethics and plagiarism. If you do a search online for recent cases of plagiarism, you may be surprised at the number of famous authors you find who have been accused of plagiarism. Often, when the allegations are proven true, the only defense that the author can provide is that they took poor notes, and as they wrote, they confused their original ideas with what was borrowed from others. As in many things, ignorance and error are not excuses for poor behavior. It is your responsibility, as a researcher and writer, to take careful notes and ensure that all source material is properly credited.

**Summary**

Effective research includes choosing a good topic, developing a working outline, finding sources and determining their credibility, taking useful notes, and ensuring that you give credit where credit is due. Each of these is an important foundation in the writing process, and glossing over any step can make writing a more difficult experience. But if you follow a process, one that works for you, and you keep careful notes and records, the actual writing of your document will go much more smoothly.

# CHAPTER 5

# The Writing Process

*When something can be read without effort,*
*great effort has gone into its writing.*
*~Enrique Jardiel Poncela*

# Chapter 5: The Writing Process

## Introduction

Some writers, mostly those who are inexperienced yet have some level of natural talent, do not believe in rough drafts. They feel that what comes out first is their best work, and other than changing a comma here and there, they believe it is good to go as is. But for most of these writers, and for all writers in general, this is not an accurate assessment of our first writing drafts. Most of us, no matter our skill level, begin with a rough draft that needs to be read and reread, reorganized, corrected, and improved upon. This first draft can be solid and an excellent start, but most likely it will require some level of massaging to become a fully effective and complete final draft.

So, let's walk through a rough draft. As you take your notes, per the previous chapter, you will eventually find that you are fleshing out your sections quite a bit and in fact have something that resembles a rough draft. Now, it is time to turn those notes into actual paragraphs and a true draft. Do this by opening both of your files, your original outline and your new notes. Update your outline, if you made any notes that impact it. Then, go section by section and begin writing. If you have done your note taking well, this is a relatively pain-free process – you already have sources and information, you have already captured the information in the appropriate heading. You need only turn it into well-written sentences and paragraphs.

### *Avoiding Writer's Block*

When you are working your notes into paragraph form, do not let yourself become overwhelmed. As they say, just take one step at a time, put one foot in front of the other. Work on a single section. After you have a solid rough draft of one section, then move to the next section. If you find that you are stumbling over a section and becoming aggravated, skip it  and move on for now. Never let yourself sit and stress over a part that is difficult to write; always take a break from that part and move on to something you can complete. This will help you feel accomplished again, and prepared to retry the difficult sections later. Some people find the introductions and conclusions the easiest to write because they are, essentially, summaries of the rest of the document. Generally you want to save these sections for the end, but if you feel that you are having trouble writing a section and you want to begin work on the introduction or conclusion just to get a break, go ahead and do it. Whatever you do, when you experience a block in your writing ability, do not quit. Always stop your writing when you are doing well and feel good about your accomplishment. Always leave it as a positive experience; never put your work away when you are upset, frustrated, or unaccomplished. Complete some section, edit a section, adjust your outline – do something so that you can put your writing away on a positive note, emotionally ready to tackle it again in the near future.

### *Constructing Effective Sentences and Paragraphs*

There are four basic components to any successful sentence or paragraph. Each sentence and/or paragraph should meet all of the following criteria:

- have necessary and accurate content that works toward the document's purpose
- be well organized, with good flow of ideas

- be grammatically complete and correct, including proper spelling and punctuation
- be easy for the audience to read

You can ensure proper grammar and good punctuation by reviewing a grammar text, as recommended in Chapter 3. Most grammar texts will also provide information on sentence structure and organization. But we will discuss a few specific tips and guidelines here.

A well-constructed sentence flows well, uses language the audience understands, is clear and is easy to read. When you work hard to construct solid sentences and paragraphs, you make your readers' job easier, which should be a major goal. Each sentence should house just one idea or related sub-ideas. Similarly, paragraphs should cover just one topic or sub-topic, all with related ideas. If you are changing ideas completely, begin a new paragraph.

Try not to begin a paragraph with words such as, "However," "But," or other similar conjunctions and qualifiers. Doing so makes that paragraph dependant upon the previous paragraph, whereas every paragraph should stand alone with its own ideas stated completely. When you do have a paragraph with numerous ideas that are different but related, be sure to guide the reader on your path. One effective way of doing this is to start with information the reader knows and use that to lead to new information. For example, consider the following paragraph:

> When building a personal computer, there are a number of common components that should be selected first. Motherboards are the backbone of any computer system, as they house the connections and slots for all other components. If processing power is of great importance, then it may be best to choose the Central Processing Unit (CPU) first, then choose a motherboard that accepts it.

After reading the above paragraph, ask yourself, does this read clearly? It is a simple paragraph, no difficult concepts to understand, so you probably got the main idea. However, if you look at it closely you will see that it does not flow very well. The sentences are disjointed, and a novice computer user might be confused by the apparent jump from discussing building a computer in general to motherboards to CPUs, with no transition between ideas. Consider instead the following version:

> When building a personal computer, there are a number of common components that should be selected first. Choosing the motherboard first is usually best because motherboards are the backbone of any computer system, as they house the connections and slots for all other components. However, if processing power is of great importance, then it may be best to choose the Central Processing Unit (CPU) first, then choose a motherboard that accepts it.

Notice that with this second paragraph, the ideas flow from one to the next. It begins by saying there are components that should come first. The second sentence begins with the idea that choosing a motherboard first is often best. The two ideas are logically related and sequential. The third sentence is then connected by the word "However", which lets the reader know that an alternate course of action is about to be suggested, giving them an insight into the sentence.

When you write paragraphs, it is important to read them carefully, preferably out loud, to ensure that each sentence flows into the next and that paragraphs are well organized and easy to read. Avoid excessive use of pronouns, which can be unclear, and ensure that any modifying words are clear as to what words they are modifying.

### Other Reminders

As you write your paper, keep in mind your audience, purpose, and any requirements. Occasionally read back over the notes you made at the top of your paper to be sure you are staying on track.

Track your sources carefully, not just within the text as discussed previously, but also in a full list of references that will eventually appear at the end of your document. Track every author, date, title, and Web retrieval or publisher information. Do not save this task for the end or you will end up running around, trying to find your sources again; a very frustrating task. Build your reference list as you go, source by source, and you will be in great shape when you wrap up your writing and create your final reference list.

## Revising

So, you have spent hours, maybe days, even weeks researching and researching, taking note after note, and writing, writing, writing. Finally, you have a solid rough draft. Now you have to revise it, to polish it into a complete, readable draft that is ready for delivery.

When revising, there are four main areas to consider: content, organization, readability, and grammar. The order these were listed is also the most logical order to revise in. It would make little sense to spend time fixing numerous commas in a paragraph that you end up deleting because it does not fit your content. First things first; fix the big issues in content and organization, then work on the readability of each sentence and paragraph, including punctuation and grammar.

### Revising the Big Picture

As noted above, the first areas that should be addressed in a revision are the global issues, where you look at the "big picture" of your paper, ignoring details for now. These global issues include content and organization concerns.

Content refers to the actual information in your paper. This is closely related to purpose; to review the content you need to consider whether you covered all of the information necessary to accomplish your purpose, and ensure that you did not cover information that does not belong. You have to be able to look back at your purpose, as well as your audience and requirements, and feel confident that you have stayed true to each. When reviewing content, consider the following questions:

- Does the document cover every aspect of the directions or requirements?
- Does it meet the intended purpose?
- Does it provide all of the information that the intended audience needs to know?
- Is there any extraneous information that does not belong?

If you find you have extra information that is not necessary, delete it. If you find you are missing some ideas that should be included, then go back to your research and add what is necessary. Once you are confident that the content is there and solid, you can move on to the next revision topic, organization.

Organization refers to the logical sequence of information as it is presented in a document. A good document has a logical flow; ideas move easily from one to the next, taking the reader along on an easy journey, requiring no jumps in logic or questioning on the part of the reader. A good paper introduces its topic, then moves through each item, one by one. Relating ideas together and finally coming full circle to a logical conclusion or summary.

For many, reviewing organization is most easily done in printed form, with pen in hand. In this fashion it is easy to draw lines between ideas, arrows moving one paragraph before another and other complicated mark-ups that would be challenging on computer. In Figure 5.1 is an example of a rough draft that has been printed, then marked up, looking at the "big picture", global organization issues. At this point, grammar and punctuation is not yet being reviewed.

*Leading Diverse Teams*

*Do I need to explain climate more than the next sentence does?*

*add more*

Leading teams can be challenging under the best circumstances but can be even more so in the current professional climate. No longer do teams consist of the three people who are geographically closest and physically similar to you. Today's office team can consist of people who are geographically and demographically diverse; 'distributed teams' is a new buzzword in information technology and other fields. Leading such a team can take some extra effort, but it can also be very rewarding, both personally, and professionally. When working in diverse teams, you have access to more ideas, more suggestions, and more creativity than you have probably had before. By managing your team properly it can be less susceptible to group think, and more likely to be productive beyond your goals. The key to leading diverse teams begins with getting to know and understand your team.

Once your team begins work, your job really begins. Communicate with each member in your group regularly. Ask them how they are progressing on their tasks, and how they see their tasks fitting in with the larger team goal. Look for any potential communications problems by mentally comparing the reports of each team member, and ensuring that everyone is thinking along the same lines. If you work in close concert with your team, make yourself available to answer questions and solve problems, and pay attention to the communications of all members, you will probably find that your group works well together, in an environment of respect and productivity.

Begin your initial team endeavor with a get-to-know-you session, where everyone gets together and becomes familiar with each other. This may involve a few minutes talking about the kids, or the new house, but more importantly, it involves having every group member tell a bit about themselves, professionally, and about their goals and ideas for the project. Through this initial meeting, you will ensure that everyone understands the project goals, and has a sense of the process. You will also gain valuable ideas about how to proceed, and may even decided on a new direction, other than what you had envisioned before the meeting. Use this time to gather information on each team member's strengths and weakness, and use that to assign sub-teams or specific tasks. Use this meeting to set your expectations for the group as far as group dynamics. Explain to your team the benefits of working on this team, and tell them how you expect them to utilize the diverse resources of the group.

*→ make this last paragraph.*

Figure 5.1: Rough Draft, Marked for Organization

*Fine-Tuning the Details*

Once you have your content set and a solid order established, you can work on readability. In reality, readability is related to organization, and by fixing the organization you have already repaired many readability issues, so you are now a step ahead on this one. You can focus on ensuring that your language is audience appropriate, that your sentences lead the reader easily through the information, and that questions which occur to the reader are answered as they move through the document. One method to revise for readability is to read your document out loud. This is an excellent way to catch awkward phrases or any issues that could cause a reader to get hung up. If at any point you question the meaning of a word or phrase, stop and fix it. If you, as author, have even the faintest question about the document, the reader will likely be very confused.

Finally, the moment you have been waiting for – grammar. This is the final step on the road to polishing your rough draft. And, lucky you, your handy-dandy computer can take on the lion's share of this task. Start by running your word processor's spell-check program and correcting any errors that you find. Next, run grammar-check and take a look at the issues your word processor brings to your attention. Be careful with computer grammar checks; they are not always completely accurate. But they can be excellent tools.

When fine-tuning your paper, there are a number of good tips to remember and implement, as follows:

- Use your word processor's spell and grammar checks.
- Print your document for the final proofread.
- Read your document out loud.
- Read backwards, starting at the end of a page, read each word, but in reverse order. Reading words out of context will help you catch spelling errors that your word processor missed.
- Have your paper reviewed by a peer, if possible.

Also, look at each sentence, noticing and correcting any of the following problems:

- long, run-on sentences
- awkward sentences that force the reader to reread and guess their meaning
- fragments, those which are not grammatically complete sentences
- sentences with too many ideas that are hard to read
- paragraphs with too many ideas that do not flow well
- consistency in voice and tense
- sexist language
- abstract words or slang
- excessive wordiness
- overdone writing, that which is vague, pompous, or simply more difficult to read than necessary

One item that could go on either of the above lists, as either a positive to add or a negative to delete, is repetition. There is an old saying in public speaking, "Tell them what you are going to tell them, then tell them, then tell them what you just said." This refers to the idea of introducing a reader to a topic, explaining the topic in detail, then summarizing the topic. In some ways it can seem repetitive. But then again, even the best writing does not always hold a reader's strict attention, beginning to end, so a little repetition could go a long way toward getting an important point or idea across[14]. When you proofread, check your writing for such repetition, then ask yourself if the repetition is necessary and helpful to the reader, or extraneous and potentially annoying. Remember that writing is an art, not a science, and you must often make judgment calls to the best of your ability.

Figure 5.2 shows the previous excerpt on Leading Diverse Teams. This time the organization issues have been corrected, and this mark-up focuses on fine-tuning grammar, word choice, and punctuation.

*Leading Diverse Teams*

Leading teams can be challenging under the best circumstances, but can be even more so in the current professional climate, where companies and workers are often geographically distributed. No longer do teams consist of the three people who are geographically closest and physically similar to you. Today's office team can consist of people who are geographically and demographically diverse; 'distributed teams' is a new buzzword in information technology and other fields, referring to teams where the members do not work in the same location. Leading such a team can take some extra effort, but it can also be very rewarding, both personally, and professionally. When working in diverse teams, you have access to more ideas, more suggestions, and more creativity than you have probably had before. By managing your team properly, it can be less susceptible to group think, and more likely to be productive beyond your goals. The key to leading diverse teams begins with getting to know and understand your team *members / the team*.

Begin your initial team endeavor with a get-to-know-you session, where everyone gets together and becomes familiar with each other. *Effectively* This may involve a few minutes talking about the kids, or the new house, but more importantly, it involves having every group member tell a bit about themselves, professionally, and about their goals and ideas for the project. Through this initial meeting, you will ensure that everyone understands the project goals, and has a sense of the process. You will also gain valuable ideas about how to proceed, and may even decide on a new direction, other than what you had envisioned before the meeting. Use this time to gather information on each team member's strengths and weakness, and use that to assign sub-teams or specific tasks. Use this meeting to set your expectations for the group as far as group dynamics. Explain to your team the benefits of working on this team, and tell them how you expect them to utilize the diverse resources of the group.

Once your team *starts* begins work, your job really begins. Communicate with each member in your group regularly. Ask them how they are progressing on their tasks, and how they see their tasks fitting in with the larger team goal. Look for any potential communications problems by mentally comparing the reports of each team member, and *of* ensuring that everyone is thinking along the same lines. If you work in close concert with your team, make yourself available to answer questions and solve problems, and pay attention to the communications of all members, you will probably find that your group works well together, in an environment of respect and productivity.

Figure 5.2: Rough Draft, Marked for Grammar and Punctuation

---

[14] You may have seen that used in this text; some important ideas are repeated in slightly different ways, or you, the reader, are directed back to them at various points.

After you have fixed your major organizational issues and corrected your grammar and punctuation, it is time for that last check. Read back over your requirements and ensure that you hit upon everything. Ask yourself the following questions:

- Is the tone of this document appropriate to my audience?
- Does this paper satisfy the purpose of the writing?
- Did I meet all requirements and guidelines?

Next, double-check your citations; ensure that you have cited everything clearly and accurately, and that every source used in your document is cited in full at the end of your paper, and vice versa. Lastly, attach any front-matter such as cover page, acknowledgments, table of contents, abstract, etc. If you have any supporting appendices, add those on the back. If you convert your file to .pdf or some other file type, always give a good look over the document after the conversion to ensure that no problems have surfaced in the look or layout.

## Summary

Good writing begins with an outline, as covered in Chapter 4, then moves easily to a rough draft. Do not feel as though you have to write the document in order, as forcing yourself to push through a difficult section can cause unease and the dreaded writer's block. Rather, feel free to move between sections, writing what interests you at the time, and go back to other sections later. As you write, construct well-organized, logical sentences that flow and are easy for the audience to read. Avoid awkward word choices or slang. Once you have a solid draft with all sections filled out, it is time to proofread and revise. Begin by looking for major organizational issues – the big picture. Correct these problems before moving on to fine-tuning grammar and punctuation. Follow these steps and creating a solid paper will be a much less stressful experience.

# CHAPTER 6

# Document Types and Formatting

*To write well, express yourself like common people,*
*but think like a wise man. Or, think as wise men do,*
*but speak as the common people do.*
*~Aristotle*

# Chapter 6: Document Types and Formatting

## Introduction

The first aspect of a paper that your audience will notice is the format and organization. A poorly formatted paper, one that uses a difficult-to-read font, has insufficient white space, lacks headings, or does not seem appropriately laid out for the purpose it is to serve makes a bad first impression and does not encourage the reader to continue. Your paper can contain the most amazingly insightful information ever to grace a page, but if it is not attractively presented and effectively organized, the ideas may be lost to the reader, rendering the paper ineffective.

There are many different types of writing and various purposes. For some types, there are common formats, even templates,. Letters, resumes, proposals, and progress report, for example, tend to follow specific guidelines and include much the same information, no matter what the topic. Other documents, such as technical manuals, research papers, descriptions, and white papers, do not necessarily follow a set pattern, and thus it is important for the writer to understand and apply basic standards for formatting and organization. Most business and IT professionals will spend much of their time writing e-mails, letters, memos, and other such brief, often relatively casual, documents. But depending upon your specific job, you may write more formal documents, such as white papers, research papers, and proposals.

The mission of this text is not to provide you with standardized templates, where you need only fill in the blank, but rather to help you learn to develop well-written, properly organized, effectively formatted writing that suits the needs of whatever document you are creating. In this chapter, we will present an overview of some common types of writing noted above, specifically, the research paper, proposal, and progress report. We will also cover the development of informative and concise abstracts and executive summaries. Note that one major type of writing, correspondence (including letters and e-mail), is covered in Chapter 7.

## Research papers

Research papers are just that, documents that provide an overview of research on a specific topic, generally in an effort to teach the reader or to showcase the knowledge of the writer, as is often the case in academic writing. Research papers generally make use of source material including journal articles, books, and Web sites, with all sources cited. The format for a research paper can vary depending on for whom the paper is being written. The writer may be asked to use a specific formatting style, such as APA or MLA. But in general a research paper contains a cover page, abstract, table of contents, body, and a reference list or bibliography. If you are writing a paper and no format is specified, just be sure to format the document in an easy-to-read manner that allows enough white space to be easy on a reader's eyes and provides basic citation information such as the sources name, copyright date, and publishing or retrieval information. Other than the basics listed above, the sections of a research paper will vary greatly depending upon the outline of the paper. As with any document, when writing a research paper you should keep in mind your target audience, the intended purpose, and any specific guidelines or requirements.

## Proposals

Similar to research papers, proposals can vary greatly in design, layout, and length. However, brief proposals do tend to be more formulated than a research paper. When you think of a proposal a wide range of possibilities come to mind. A proposal can be a monumental undertaking. For example, a grant proposal, attempting to solicit money for an organization to conduct research, can be very long and detailed. Such proposals can be tens of pages long and filled with incredible detail. But most proposals written in the business world are of a more simple type, and can be brief, perhaps 1-2 pages. Whatever the length, there is a basic format that one can follow when creating a proposal.

The basic format is simple. A proposal is generally written in a memo format (though larger-scale proposals will have cover pages instead) and includes the following sections:

- The proposal begins with a summary that overviews the situation which necessitated a request of some sort, then summarizes the request itself (the proposal).
- The document then provides details, generally including the following sections: Background of Problem, Proposed Solution, Conclusion. In a detailed proposal there may be many subsections to each of these headings, but these are the basics.

The first section is an introduction or summary. An introduction is usually brief, just introducing what is to come in your proposal in a concise way. A summary is generally considered more effective. With a summary, you thoroughly overview the entire proposal, briefly providing the background of the problem and the solution you are proposing.

When writing proposals, be sure to keep the audience in mind, as with all writing. The proposal should be well written, properly organized and formatted, free of spelling and punctuation errors, and grammatically correct. Proofread it. Then proofread it again. It is a good idea to print your paper and read the hard copy, red pen in hand. See tips on proofreading and revising in Chapter 5. Remember that you want your audience to approve your proposal, and to achieve this you must show yourself to be reliable, thorough and credible.

The following pages show an example of a brief, well-written proposal. Note that the proposal begins with a summary, which briefly overviews the entire proposal. It then continues with the sections, as described above, and ends with a conclusion that restates the proposal and indicates that the writer is waiting for approval of the project. Remember that a proposal is just that, a request to be allowed to do something. Thus, a proposal should always request a specific action from the audience.

Date:  February 12, 2007
To:    Professor of Introduction to Information Technology Course
From:  Mark Jankowski
Re:    Proposal to create an instructional paper on migrating to Microsoft
       Windows New Operating System

## Summary

Microsoft Windows has recently released the next generation of the Windows Operating System, Windows X.  Within several months, Information Technology (IT) professionals will begin their planning stages to migrate to the new operating system (OS). I propose the development of a paper that will examine the new features in the OS that are tailored to an IT professional, such as security enhancements, the ability to roll out the OS to computers using cloning technology, and migrating user data. In addition, the paper will propose strategies and necessary steps that an IT professional has to perform in order to complete successful migration to Microsoft Windows X.

## Problem

Microsoft Windows X is a new OS that is being released to the public. However, many IT professionals lack information and knowledge to migrate to Windows X.  Without a migration plan and knowledge of the new Microsoft Windows OS, an IT professional does not have the means to accomplish their mission. Additionally, there are several new features, tools, and security enhancements IT professionals will be unaware of if they do not have the proper knowledge.

## Solution

To solve the issue of many IT professionals lacking information and knowledge to migrate to the new Windows OS, I will develop a paper that will provide accurate and detailed information on the tools, steps, and security features that are needed to migrate to the new OS.  The topics that will be included are:
- Planning and Designing Deployments

- Cloning Techniques and Tools

- Security

- Managing Microsoft Windows X

## Timeline for Completion

The table on the following page provides a timeline for completing the major milestones throughout this project.

| Task | Start Date | End Date |
|---|---|---|
| Project Research and Planning | January 15 | January 28 |
| Draft Outline | January 21 | January 27 |
| Project Proposal | February 12 | February 18 |
| Draft Paper | January 25 | March 5 |
| Progress Report | March 2 | March 5 |
| Initial Edits and Revisions | March 5 | March 11 |
| Feedback from Peers | March 11 | March 12 |
| Finalize Paper (Edits and Revisions) | March 13 | March 18 |
| Final Submission | March 18 | March 18 |

Table 1: Timeline

## Conclusion

Microsoft Windows X is a massive upgrade from previous Windows operating systems, and IT professionals need to be properly trained on the tools and steps to migrate to the new OS. Without the proper knowledge of Microsoft Windows X, a lot of money and manpower will be needlessly spent migrating to the new Windows OS. With knowledge of the new OS, IT professionals will have no difficulties migrating because they will have the ability to create a migration plan and use the tools that are provided to them. The proposed paper will be completed no later than March 18, 2007. I look forward to your response indicating that I may proceed with development of this paper.

Figure 6.1: Sample Proposal (adapted from Jankowski, 2007)

## Progress Report

Often when working on a large project, you will be asked to submit one or more progress reports as the project progresses. A progress report is not only often a required component of a large project, but also can be a valuable tool for the author. This type of report functions to tell how well a project is progressing. This information can be effective for management, as it informs them how well you are working and when they can expect results. It is also effective for the creator, as developing even a brief progress report helps you put your thoughts in order and see what work you have left to do.

Progress reports should be attractive, well organized and written, and easy to skim over. They should have clear sections headings, and include at least the following information:

- a recap of the problem and the proposed solution
  (This recap is necessary because often the person reviewing your progress report — your boss, your teacher, the company president — has many other projects they are overseeing at the same time. It is important that you provide this brief recap to refresh their memory of what your project is about and what the purpose of the project is.)
- Discussion of how project is going
  (This is the "meat" of the progress report. In this section you describe what you have done and what is left to do. You describe whether your project is on time per your original time table, if it is on budget, etc.).
- Description of any problems that were encountered and how they were solved or will be solved
  (This section discusses any problems, setbacks, or complications that you have experienced in working on your project and how it impacts your project. It also tells how you solved or will solve the problem, how you will get the project back on track, and includes a new due date if applicable).
- Conclusion
  (Every paper you every write should have a conclusion, and this is no exception. Your conclusion will briefly restate what you are doing and how it is going, ending with a statement that you are either on schedule, that you will get on schedule, or reiterating your new schedule).

Your progress report should be written in memo form, similar to a proposal, indicating the date, your name, the name of the person you are writing it to and the topic of the proposal. Note that proposals and progress reports can be written in first or third person, as appropriate. If the work is to be done by a team, then third person is used. If the work is to be done independently, first person is acceptable, as is used in the samples of this chapter.

The example on the following pages is a progress report, detailing progress made on the same paper proposed in the previous example.

Date:   March 5, 2007
To:      Professor of Introduction to Information Technology Course
From:  Mark Jankowski
Subject: Progress Report on creation of instructional paper on migrating to Microsoft
            Windows X

## Summary

The purpose of this message is to report the progress made on development of the paper, "Migrating to Microsoft Windows X." This report details the activities from January 8 to February 27. My paper will provide valuable information and knowledge to Information Technology (IT) professionals on how to migrate to the new Windows Operating System (OS) using a migration plan. In this paper, IT professionals will learn how to protect a Windows X OS, image computers using cloning technology, and migrate user data. Overall, the paper development is going smoothly and I expect to submit the paper by the agreed-upon due date of March 18, 2007.

## Problems

Research and writing of the paper is going well. The only problem I have encountered with the project thus far is the overall length of the paper.  I had too much information to incorporate into the final paper, thus I used feedback from my project proposal to shorten my outline. Specifically, I removed a topic from my outline that discussed training end users on Windows X. By shortening my outline, the paper will be in the page limitation that was set forth in the project requirements.

## Progress

The table below provides information on my progress thus far as well as the steps that need to be completed before posting the final paper.

| Task | Percentage Complete | Next Steps Before Posting |
|---|---|---|
| Project Research and Planning | 100% | |
| Draft Outline | 100% | |
| Project Proposal | 100% | |
| Draft Paper | 85% | |
| Progress Report | 100% | Incorporate Feedback and Revisions |
| Initial Edits and Revisions | 0% | Revisions |
| Feedback from Peers | 0% | Incorporate Feedback and Revisions |
| Finalize Paper (Edits and Revisions) | 0% | Incorporate Feedback and Revisions |
| Final Submission | 0% | Incorporate Feedback and Revisions |

Figure 1: Progress Detail

My current schedule has me completing my rough draft by March 1, 2007, to submit for peer review. Once I have received feedback, I will finalize my rough draft for submission.

## Conclusion

Migrating to Microsoft Windows X is a massive undertaking.  The paper I am writing will provide IT professionals with the knowledge to use the tools and steps to migrate to Windows X. Since I began work on this project, I have maintained a steady workflow and completed each step of the project on time.  I am very pleased with the progress of work that has been completed thus far.  I am on schedule and open for any suggestions or modifications to the paper before I finalize the rough draft for submission on March 18, 2007.

Figure 6.2: Sample Progress Report (adapted from Jankowski, 2007)

## Abstracts and Executive Summaries

Most lengthy papers, specifically journal articles, white papers, and research papers, will have an abstract or executive summary. An abstract is a summary of the major points in a paper presented in a concise way. An abstract is complete enough that it tells a reader if the paper's content is of interest to and pertinent to them, and at least presents the major points that will be covered. An abstract should be about one paragraph of 200-300 words. An executive summary is similar to an abstract but is usually more complete, more thoroughly summarizing all of the major points in the paper. An executive summary should be so complete that it can actually be read instead of the paper, as it hits all major topics. Abstracts are used more often than executive summaries, as they are more brief and thus more useful to the reader.

When writing an abstract or an executive summary, use all of the tenants of good writing that we have discussed throughout this book[15]. Be concise. Write clearly. Remember your audience, and choose audience-appropriate words. Ensure that your sentences flow from one to the next in both ideas and grammar.

Figure 6.3 on the following page is an example of an abstract on the completed paper that was used in the previous examples. Note that an executive summary would be similar, but would instead simply break into a sentence or so of further detail on each of the areas mentioned in the abstract.

---

[15] At this point you may have noticed that this text moves from first person ("I" and "we") to second person ("you") and even third person ("the text") occasionally. In general, when writing professional documents you will choose one form (first, second or third person), and stick with it. However, the author takes some liberties with this text as we move from discussing the general focus of the text, to specific suggestions for you to carry out, thus requiring switches from first to second and third person to best suit our purpose at that specific point.

## Abstract

Microsoft Windows X is the next generation of the Windows Operating System (OS). Within several months, Information Technology (IT) professionals will begin their planning stages to migrate to the new OS. This paper examines the new features in the OS that are tailored to an IT professional, including security enhancements, the ability to roll out the OS to computers using cloning technology, and migrating user data. This paper will include strategies and necessary steps that an IT professional must perform for a successful migration. Specifically, this document discusses that to migrate to Microsoft Windows X, a checklist of operations needs to take place. This checklist involves four main areas: defining your deployment project scope and objectives, assessing your current computing environment, testing and piloting your deployment plan, and rolling out your deployment plan. Additionally, there are many tools Microsoft has incorporated and improved in Windows X that allow you to secure your environment, many of which are overviewed in this paper. Finally, understanding that managing Windows X in a network is crucial for an IT professional, and this document covers the various tools that Microsoft has incorporated into Windows X to allow them to remotely monitor and administer the network. Some such tools Microsoft has included in Windows X are the Microsoft Management Console, Performance and Reliability Monitor, and Print Management. By creating a migration plan, an IT professional can effectively plan, evaluate, deploy, and manage a Microsoft Windows X environment and have a positive migration experience.

Figure 6.3: Sample Abstract (Adapted from Jankowski, 2007)

## Summary

Much like individual people have their own flair and style, so can documents. Following a template is not always the best way to design an effective paper. However, for some types of documents there are basic formulas that are common and work well in most situations. This chapter overviewed some basic tenants for developing effective proposals, progress reports and abstracts. If you find yourself in a situation that does not fit these formats exactly, you should feel free to alter the format so that it is appropriate to your audience and the purpose of the document, while still ensuring that it is well organized, attractively formatted, easy to read, and credible.

# CHAPTER 7

# Career and Correspondence

---

*A man who publishes his letters becomes a nudist —nothing
shields him from the world's gaze except his bare skin.
A writer, writing away, can always fix himself up to
make himself more presentable, but a man who has
written a letter is stuck with it for all time.
~E.B. White*

# Chapter 7: Career and Correspondence

## Introduction

In this chapter we cover two ideas that may seem different at first glance, yet are actually related: career (specifically, finding a job) and correspondence (letters and e-mails). These ideas are related in that a large part of finding a job involves writing an effective cover letter, and perhaps even follow-up letters. This chapter covers these ideas and more.

## Resumes

There are various formats common to resumes. Some are neat, clean and effective. Other are bad, and some are worse. But most are similar and straightforward in design. Overall, a resume should be attractive, easy to read, and lend itself to skimming, as this is what most hiring employers do. Considering that resumes are innately professional, they also are very personal documents. Accepted formats vary widely, and the final overall design is largely up to the individual. Following are a number of guidelines, that are generally applicable to most resumes:

- Use a hierarchy format (rather than chronological) — this places emphasis on what you did, not when you did it.
- Make job titles more prominent than dates — this, again, places emphasis on what you did, not when you did it.
- Use objectives only when changing fields or making use of an education with little practical experience. Generally, your objective is implicit in your past experience and the position you are applying for.
- Limit your resume to one page when possible, two pages maximum – few reviewers will take the time to read more than two pages. A resume is designed to get you an interview, not tell your life story.
- Place education at the beginning of your resume if an education is required for the position or if you received your highest degree within the last three or four years. After a few years, education generally moves to the bottom of a resume, as experience takes precedence. List only the highest degrees earned, unless the subject of the lesser degree is of particular importance.

Following is a more in-depth discussion on these, and other, resume basics.

### Resume Length

There is no law regarding resume length. It used to be said that a resume should never exceed one page. That was easy when people stayed at one job for 20 years, and thus had few positions to fill resume space. But now many workers switch jobs often, and it is not uncommon to have three, four, five or even more jobs listed on one's resume. This makes the one-page rule nearly impossible. Two pages are perfectly acceptable for a resume. Three pages may be acceptable, but know that few human resource people have the time or the inclination to sift through more than two pages. What is written in rock, however, is that you never add a page to your resume if you cannot fill at least two-thirds of the paper. If you add a page and it's only half full, either add to it or delete it.

*Resume Objectives*

An objective is designed for people who are changing fields or positions or who are just breaking into a field. Objectives are meant to show your goals when your resume might not reflect the experience those goals normally would require. Objectives can also be used for specific situations, such as someone trying to relocate or someone looking for a specific experience/employer. You can also use an objective as a place to put desired pay, if a job listing requires it.

Most job seekers do not want to use an objective, and it is perfectly fine to exclude this from a resume. However, if you feel you have something particular to state, feel free to use an objective. If you choose to use an objective, make sure it is brief, to the point, specific, and well written. Avoid generic statements that give no real information and do not differentiate you from any other applicant.

*Resume Headers and Headings*

A resume should be well written and easy to read. Its design should be attractive. One effective tool is the use of bold fonts to highlight important points. As for address headers, the traditional format was to center ones' name and address at the top of the page. This is no longer a standard. The purpose of the header is simply to allow you to be easily identified and contacted. This information, while it should always appear prominently at the top of each page, can be formatted however you wish. Simply make sure that the information is printed in a clear, attractive manner.

*Resume Content*

The idea behind a resume is to prove to a potential employer that you are worthy of an interview. Your resume should not tell everything about you, but should give enough information to convince a potential employer that you have the skills they are looking for and that you are someone they want to meet. Resumes should also be honest. Sure, you are going to embellish a bit, make yourself look good – who doesn't? But do not write that you are proficient in MS Access when in reality you only opened the program once.

*Resume Grammar*

Whether you are applying for a communications position or a job selling hot dogs on a street corner, how you speak is important. Your writing should reflect your verbal grammar and should be both professional and proper. That's not to say that you need to speak like an English teacher, but you may have some common grammar errors, in both your speaking and writing, that reflect poorly on you. For example, if you grew up in a region of the country that pronounced "wash" with an "r", ("warsh"), and you have now moved to an area that speaks differently, that might be something you want to try and change. If your entire life you have misspelled the word "necessary," thinking there were two "C's" as well as two "S's", then look the word up, write it over and over until you get it right. Remember that "ain't" is not a proper word, even if it is now in some dictionaries as slang. Get past your years of habitual grammatical errors so that you are prepared to present yourself in the best possible light to make a positive first impression.

One common mistake in resumes is not using parallel language in your descriptions. If you are describing a job you have now, all verbs should be present tense. If it is a past job, all verbs should be past tense. Be consistent. And, by all means, use many verbs – a resume full of action verbs can impart a positive emotion on a reviewer.

Grammar is the most subtle way to show who you are. Clean up your grammar, spoken and written, and you change the way people see you.

### *Resume Organization*

Similar to style, organization is the way you arrange the information in your resume. Consider this: do you still have your education listed at the top of your resume, even though you graduated in 1991? This probably no longer belongs at the top as it is not timely information, likely your experience now outweighs what you learned in college. However, if you are in school now, earning a higher degree, you may want to move the education back to the top. But when your degree is more than a few years old, it moves back down on the list. Also, as mentioned previously, tradition tells us to list jobs in chronological order, but this is no longer necessary in most job situations. In modern times, a resume should reflect your experience, not your time served. List the jobs of most interest to your potential employer first. If you worked two years as a Web designer, but the company went under and you had to work as a waitperson for a year, is your resume going to have your waitperson job at the top, obscuring your Web design experience? Probably not. As mentioned previously, when you list jobs, list your job title first, not the company name or the date. **What** you did is usually far more important than **where** or **when** you did it, and should be the most prominent information. However, there are some situations where chronological order is important, thus this type of resume will be discussed in detail.

The two main types of resume are chronological and functional. In a chronological resume, job experience is listed in date order, from most recent to oldest. As noted previously, this type of resume was common 15 and more years ago, but is less common today. However, chronological resumes are still used in applying for positions where you are required to account completely for your time from a specific date (often graduating college) until the present. Often, government agencies and contractors require such resumes. Following is an example of a chronological resume of a technical writer.

**Willow Rosenburg**

14759 Wick Road, Sunnydale, California, 98751, 555-812-1912

## Highlights of Skills

- Extensive software design experience.
- Experience working in and leading teams.
- Exceptional client relations experience.

## Experience

*Computer Science Instructor*                                    Aug. 2006 - present
Sunnydale Community College

> Teach introductory computer course in community college setting. Maintain classroom computers, including software and hardware updates. Supervise 30 college students per section, four sections a day.

*Team Leader, Software Design Team*                              June 2005 - Aug. 2006
Spike Computer Consultants
Rochester, California

> Designed software and systems to meet specific client database and data management needs. Met with clients to determine software criteria. Evaluated current computer systems. Implemented and maintained new systems. Supervised ten computer engineers.

*Software Designer*                                              Feb. 2004 - June 2005
Cryptographic Technologies
Sunnydale, California

> Worked in team environment to troubleshoot client software issues and beta test new software. Trained new team members.

*Software Development Intern*                                    June 2003 - Feb. 2004
High Stake Computer Associates
Roane, California

> Assisted software designers. Attended requirements meetings with clients. Assisted with beta testing of software systems. Worked help desk.

## Education

*Bachelor of Science in Computer Software Design*               May 2004
University of California, Los Angeles, California

Figure 7.1: Chronological Resume

Notice that in the above chronological resume format, the jobs are not necessarily listed in order of importance, as date was considered paramount. Let's say this person has been teaching for two years, but now she has decided that she is no longer happy in the community college world, and misses the hustle and bustle of daily life as a computer engineer. In short, she wants to go back into designing and maintaining software systems. If this is the case, does it make sense to place the current job as community college instructor at the top? Would it not make more sense to move the Team Leader position to the top, as those are the skills that the applicant wants to stress? Think for a minute about what other item this person might want to add to her resume. Perhaps an objective? When changing fields, an objective can be a good way to clarify your goals, especially if they may seem somewhat at odds with parts of your resume.

More common today is the functional resume. This type of resume is organized by order of importance – the job which shows experience most relevant to the position being applied for is listed first, followed by other jobs in descending order of relevance. Functional resumes can also have sub-sections in the experience section, dividing experience into specific categories. Following are two examples of functional resumes. Figure 7.2 shows a functional resume with just one overall experience section. Figure 7.3 shows a functional resume divided into sections. Such a resume might be used to apply for a position that required two separate sets of skills, for example strong writing skills and strong customer service skills. Note that in this resume, the education has been moved to the top because a Bachelor degree is required of all applicants, and thus was deemed important enough to move up for this iteration of the resume.

**Willow Rosenburg**

14759 Branch Road, Sunnydale, California, 98751, 555-812-1912

---

### Highlights of Experience

- Extensive software design experience.
- Experience working in and leading teams.
- Exceptional client relations experience.

### Computer Experience

*Team Leader, Software Design Team*　　　　　　　　　　June 2005 - Aug. 2006
Spike Computer Consultants
Rochester, California

    Designed software and systems to meet specific client database and data management needs. Met with clients to determine software criteria. Evaluated current computer systems. Implemented and maintained new systems. Supervised ten computer engineers.

*Software Designer*　　　　　　　　　　　　　　　　Feb. 2004 - June 2005
Cryptographic Technologies
Sunnydale, California

    Worked in team environment to troubleshoot client software issues and beta test new software. Trained new team members.

*Software Development Intern*　　　　　　　　　　　June 2003 - Feb. 2004
High Stake Computer Associates
Roane, California

    Assisted software designers. Attended requirements meetings with clients. Assisted with beta testing of software systems. Worked help desk.

*Computer Science Instructor*　　　　　　　　　　　Aug. 2006 - present
Sunnydale Community College

    Teach introductory computer course in community college setting. Maintain classroom computers, including software and hardware updates. Supervise 30 college students per section, four sections a day.

### Education

*Bachelor of Science in Computer Software Design*　　　　　　May 2004
University of California

Figure 7.2: Functional Resume A

## Willow Rosenburg
14759 Branch Road, Sunnydale, California, 98751, 555-812-1912

### Highlights of Experience
- Extensive software design experience.
- Experience working in and leading teams.
- Exceptional client relations experience.

### Education

*Bachelor of Science in Computer Software Design*                          May 2004
University of California

### Computer Experience

*Team Leader, Software Design Team*                          June 2005 - Aug. 2006
Spike Computer Consultants
Rochester, California
> Designed software and systems to meet specific client database and data
> management needs. Met with clients to determine software criteria. Evaluated
> current computer systems. Implemented and maintained new systems. Supervised
> ten computer engineers.

*Software Designer*                          Feb. 2004 - June 2005
Cryptographic Technologies
Sunnydale, California
> Worked in team environment to troubleshoot client software issues and beta test
> new software. Trained new team members.

*Software Development Intern*                          June 2003 - Feb. 2004
High Stake Computer Associates
Roane, California
> Assisted software designers. Attended requirements meetings with clients.
> Assisted with beta testing of software systems. Worked help desk.

### Teaching Experience

*Computer Science Instructor*                          Aug. 2006 - present
Sunnydale Community College
> Teach introductory computer course in community college setting. Maintain
> classroom computers, including software and hardware updates. Supervise 30 college
> students per section, four sections a day.

Figure 7.3: Functional Resume B

Technical Communication in the Information Age

*Resume Tip*

As discussed, opinions on resume length and design vary greatly. Furthermore, your resume will change with the type of position you are applying for or the type of company you are applying to. In some creative fields, people have been known to successfully submit outrageously formatted resumes, while in more technical fields a concise, neat, well-presented resume generally serves best. But one thing is for certain: you never know where life will take you and what previously polished skills might suddenly seem important. Thus, it is a good idea to keep a "master" resume, one that includes every job you have had throughout your life. This master resume will be just for your personal use. This way you always have the dates of every job you have had and all other information that you might need at your fingertips. You never know when an employer will want 20 years of work history; you might end up needing some type of security clearance or may just find a very thorough employer. Maybe someday you will try to get a contract designing a Web page for restaurant employees, in which case it might be good to tell them you know the ins and outs of the food business since you delivered pizzas in 1984. Keep a complete resume, then, as you apply for jobs, pick and choose from that resume what is pertinent to the position you are applying for.

There are myriad books written on resumes and job hunting. If you are seriously job hunting, it would benefit you greatly to purchase and read one of these books. They will include numerous sample resumes, more in-depth descriptions of various resumes types, sample cover letters, and even tips for successful interviewing and follow-up communications. For a list of recommended books, please see the Suggested Job Search Texts at the end of this chapter.

## Cover Letters

Some people wonder about the content difference between a resume and a cover letter. In short, a cover letter is designed to persuade, to convince the reader to review your resume. A resume is designed to inform, to tell about your experience. A cover letter should persuade the reader that you are a possible candidate, worthy of having your resume considered. Your resume should give enough information to convince them that they need to meet you for an interview.

Always use a cover letter whether you are e-mailing, faxing, or sending your resume via traditional post. The cover letter should introduce you and your resume, explain how you are qualified for the position you are seeking, and make you available for an interview.

Generally, a cover letter consists of 3-4 paragraphs, as follows:

1. Explain what position you are applying for and where you heard of the opening. This should be summed up in one paragraph.
2. Overview how you are qualified for this position – sell yourself. If possible, use the job description or posting to ensure you touch upon specific traits the employer is searching for. Give specific examples, if you can. This section can be one or two paragraphs in length.
3. A closing paragraph, restating that you are qualified for this position and making yourself available for an interview.

A cover letter is that simple. It should be concise, clear, and easy to read. Remember your audience! Likely the hiring manager or human resource person is busy reading dozens of cover letters and resumes and has only a matter of seconds to dedicate to each. Make every word count.

Figure 7.4 is an example of a cover letter from a recent mechanical engineering graduate looking for an entry level position.

**Tyler Durden**

*390 Wood Drive, Oakland, Michigan  55667*
555-831-7255; tylerdurden@papersoap.com

May 25, 2007

Personnel Manager,

Attached please find this resume as my application for the Mechanical Designer position with ABC Architectural, as posted on the Monster.com Web site.  I am a mechanical engineering graduate from Oakland University and am looking to expand my work experience in this field.  Both my work history and my academic achievements qualify me for this position, especially in the areas of communication and organization.  While I have no direct working experience with AutoCAD, I have recently begun working with it privately, and believe that I can grasp it quickly.  Additionally, my aptitude for quick learning would make me an ideal candidate for this job.

My educational background has provided me with an excellent foundation for the skills required for this position.  While attending college, two design projects stand out as being beneficial.  In a Fluid & Thermal Design class I was part of a group that designed and constructed a heat exchanger that was to be used as a recouperator.  Our design met all the criteria and was one of the most cost-efficient of all the models.  The second project was my Senior Design course.  I worked in a group of interdisciplinary engineering students on a Mural Painter.  This design allowed a computer image to be enlarged and printed on a wall.  Our project was highly regarded and complimented on its concept and design.

I have a strong work ethic and take pride in my references that attest to such.  I will make a great addition to the ABC Architectural team, and look forward to discussing my qualifications with you in person.  I can be reached by phone at (555)-831-7255 or e-mail at tylerdurden@papersoap.com.  Thank you for your time.

Sincerely,

Tyler Durden

Figure 7.4: Cover Letter (adapted from Snarski, 2007)

Note that the writer uses the name of the company in the first and last paragraphs. Avoid phrases such as "your company;" always refer to the company specifically by name. By using the company name, you show a certain level of interest and dedication that generic cover letters do not. Also, if possible, learn the name of the person who is doing the hiring and address the cover letter specifically to them.

## Follow-Up and Thank You Letters

Follow-up and thank you letters are aspects of job hunting that many people, unfortunately, overlook. In today's competitive job market, you will often be competing against others who are similarly qualified, and thus you need to do your best to make yourself stand out. Having an attractive, eye-catching, modern resume is a way to make you stand out and get you an interview. Sending a follow-up or thank you letter after the interview can be an effective way to put yourself into the forefront of the interviewer's mind. It can also be a way for you to get in a little more information, or make up for something that you may have lacked in the interview.

One example of an effective use of a follow-up letter is as follows: Recently an engineering professional was trying to find a job in a very competitive market. He was granted an interview for a position that he was excited about. The interview went well, except for one potential area. The job applicant was asked if he had experience in a certain computer program the company used. He did not. He did a good job of describing how he was computer literate and a quick learner, trying to make his lack of specific experience in this area a minor issue. However, as he left the interview he felt uneasy, as though the interviewer had liked him, but had been concerned over his lack of experience in the one program. Upon returning home, the applicant called a friend who had this software installed on his laptop, and he borrowed the laptop. The applicant spent a number of hours working on the software and asked the friend for some tips. After a time he felt confident that he at least had a basic understanding of the software and felt certain that it was something he could quickly learn.

But then the applicant wondered, what would it matter that he learned the software if he did not get the job? He decided to write a follow-up letter to his interview in which he thanked the interviewer for his time and assured him that he was capable of, and eager to perform, the duties of the position. He also told the interviewer that he had procured a copy of the software the interviewer had mentioned, explaining that he had familiarized himself with the program and was completely confident that he could learn it quickly. He sent the letter via e-mail, the method of communication that the interviewer had used in scheduling the interview. A week later the applicant was called back for a second interview, at which time he was given the job.

You might ask, "How can you know the follow-up letter is what made the difference"? Well, you can't. But certainly it did not hurt, as the applicant was given the job. In fact, the follow-up letter may have made all of the difference in getting a job where many similarly qualified people were applying – this particular applicant showed a certain follow-through and commitment that most employers respect greatly.

As far as format on a follow-up or thank you letter, it is similar to the cover letter. The first paragraph reintroduces yourself and says that you enjoyed your interview with whomever on whatever day. The next paragraph reiterates how and why you are qualified for the position, if possible calling out specifics from the interview, as was done in the above story. The final paragraph says that you are enthusiastic about working for this company and that you are the person for the job, finally making yourself available for further questions.

## E-mail

Cover letters and follow-ups are two common ways you correspond with others, but there are, of course, many more. Correspondence used to mean letters either hand written or typed, and generally sent in an envelope through the postal system. Such letters included cover letters with resumes, as well as personal letters sent to friends and family, political letters sent to government officials, and even letters of compliment or criticism sent to businesses. In grade school you were likely taught the accepted format for such letters – where to place the address, how to word the salutation and such – at the same time you were taught to address and stamp envelopes. But this type of physical correspondence has largely fallen by the wayside. Few of us actually send letters through the postal service anymore other than paying bills. One of the greatest strides that communications has made in recent years is the ability to communicate instantly with electronic mail – e-mail.

E-mail is an excellent tool, allowing us to communicate with someone for essentially no money, across any distance, and without concern for time zones. E-mail lets us send files as attachments, forward funny thoughts to break up our coworkers' day, and document important conversations. For some, e-mail is a tool to keep in touch with friends and family. For others, it helps them conduct business. But whatever the purpose, most people use e-mail in a very casual way, not according it the same status that we once did actual paper letters. In actuality, the permanence of e-mail, the ability to forward it to others, the accountability that is implicit in electronic mail, help indicate that e-mail should be treated with even more attention to detail than old-fashioned hand-written letters.

One of the main problems with e-mail is that people sometimes forget that e-mail, when used in the work place, is a professional tool to be respected. Oddly, we often think of e-mail as a casual communications medium, even more casual than the telephone. Things that a person would never say, or at least say a certain way, to a person's face or on the phone, they will write in e-mail. We'll let our temper show in an e-mail, or our humor, or even our sexuality. The curious thing is, because e-mail can be saved, forwarded, and copied easily, it should actually be treated with **more** respect than other communications mediums.

One interesting aspect of e-mail is that sometimes two individuals in an office sit no more than 20 feet from each other, but still fail to communicate verbally because they choose to rely on e-mail communications. This has become all too common in the workplace, and even among personal friends. E-mail, in its purest form, is intended to facilitate communications over boundaries of time and distance. However, it has quickly been distorted in its use. Sometimes we use e-mail to communicate even with those in close proximity simply because we want written documentation of a discussion. This is fine. However, often we use e-mail to communicate with people when we are too lazy to walk 10 feet or 1 floor, or we use it to communicate with people when we do not want to face them for one reason or another. Using e-mail in this way is often not effective. Always choose your communications method (e-mail, telephone, face-to-face, or written letter) for maximum effectiveness.

## *Formatting E-mail and Attachments*

Professional e-mails should be well written, concise, and contain salutations. They should have meaningful subjects in the subject line. You should take care not to write e-mail in anger or in a rush. E-mails should be proofread and spell checked. And as an ethical consideration, always be careful of what you forward. Look over a message, making sure there is nothing personal or inappropriate embedded five pages down in an e-mail that you are about to forward to your boss. When you send e-mails to many people, consider putting the e-mail addresses in the BCC box, rather than the TO box. In this way you can keep people's e-mail addresses private when sending mass e-mails. Similarly, be respectful when replying to e-mail. Avoid using the "Reply All" tab unless your response truly is intended for, and necessary to, all original recipients.

One area of e-mail that is often overlooked is subject lines. Subject lines indicate what is to come and help separate unimportant mail from important mail. May people get dozens, if not hundreds, of e-mails every day. Often these are sorted simply by looking at the sender or subject line. Sometimes the subject line is the only thing that keeps important e-mail from getting deleted.

Furthermore, be judicious in your use of attachments. Many of today's computer systems are highly vulnerable to computer viruses and worms, and thus computer users have become suspicious of e-mail attachments. When you attach a file, always give the file a descriptive and accurate name. Also, introduce the file, tell the receiver what you are attaching so that they know that it is from you and safe to open.

## *Tone and Language*

One of the biggest challenges inherent to e-mail is the conveying of tone and emotion. Without the context that body language and voice can provide, e-mails can often be misread or misunderstood. That is why emoticons (the punctuation-based symbols for smiley faces and other emotional illustrations) developed, In personal settings, such emoticons, as well as acronyms, can be very useful. Most of us know that LOL means laugh out loud, indicating that something was funny or is intended to be taken humorously, and that  :-) represents a face smiling, and similarly indicates positive emotions associated with what has been written. But in a professional setting, it is not always appropriate to indicate tone through such informal acronyms and emoticons. Thus, you must choose your words carefully and proofread your writing to ensure that you have conveyed the intended tone.

One serious problem with e-mail is that people use it negatively, often responding quickly and in an angry manner, without taking the time to think the situation through. When you receive an e-mail communication that upsets you, never respond immediately. Following are a few tips to keep in mind when you receive an upsetting e-mail:

- Never attack the person writing the message, only the problem.
- Frame your reply in a mutually beneficial way; put a positive spin on the situation.
- Find a solution rather than placing blame.
- Never reply just to vent and fight.

- Always take time to consider your response; never write back while still angry.
- Choose your battles carefully and consider if this is truly an issue worth arguing over.

Following are examples of a poor e-mails, sent between a boss and an employee. Apparently, the boss was having issues with a long-standing employee's recent work patterns. Rather than confronting the issue face-to-face, the boss sent an e-mail. Now, in such an example, sending an e-mail **after** a conversation is a good way to document the situation and ensure that both parties viewed the conversation the same way. But to send only an e-mail is not a particularly effective method of management in this case. Figure 7.5 is the initial message from the boss to the employee.

---

Subject: (left blank)

Good Morning Allie,

Yesterday I was walking by the front counter and noticed that there was a line of customers waiting to be served. John was helping one customer, and Sara was on the phone with another. As I walked by I saw you look up, notice the line, then put your head down as if to avoid it. This type of behavior is not and will not be acceptable.

Allie, since you transitioned to your new position your co-workers and I have been very supportive. Maria has picked up many of your duties to make your transition easier, and I have helped whenever I can. But it is time for you to step up and start taking charge of the work assigned to your position. Allie, effective immediately and until further notice you will do the following:
    1. Send me a daily e-mail listing the work that you have for that day.
    2. Assist at the counter when needed, without being asked.
    3. Refrain from addressing your personal e-mail, or surfing the Internet, except
       on your lunch.

Should you choose to respond to this e-mail, you may tell me how you intend to address what I have outlined here. I do not want you to send excuses. Please know that I am not placing this in your personnel file.

Thank you,

Ms. Winters

---

Figure 7.5: Ineffective E-mail – Supervisor to Employee

When you read over this e-mail, ask yourself, what did the supervisor do wrong here? Given what the manager observed and apparently was told by others, the content of her message seems acceptable. She pointed out a problem that she saw, namely Allie ignoring customers that needed help, and suggested a course of action, specifically that Allie help at the front desk when she saw a line. This seems reasonable. What of her tone? She is a bit abrupt, but does manage to keep her tone from being mean. What about the format? The message is grammatically well written, and it is formatted in a way to be easy to read. But then, with all of these positives, can you see anything wrong with this message?

Consider this….
The message specifically spells out that the employee did not help customers at the front desk when she should have. However, it also implies that there were some other past issues that are not addressed in this letter. Thus, the message is incomplete, and seems to be a small part of a larger problem that is not adequately addressed here, and does not appear to have been brought to the employee's attention before. Also, by mentioning other employees by name, she creates a potentially awkward working situation. Finally, the supervisor comes across as very negative with the line about not wanting to read excuses. In all, the message may be grammatically well written, but this supervisor seems to have some issues with proper management strategies and over-reliance of e-mail when face-to-face communications are called for.

So, we have decided that the supervisor's e-mail to the employee was not all bad, but it did have some serious issues that the supervisor should have thought better of before sending the message[16]. Now, let's look at the employee's response to the supervisor's e-mail, as shown in Figure 7.6.

Subject: I disagree

I disagree with the observation that you noted. Yesterday I worked the entire lunch
hour alone while Sara sat at her desk e-mailing her boyfriend, and John went on break.. If you look, you will find that most of yesterday's work was processed and signed by me, and that I was at the front desk almost the entire day. At the time that you walked by, I did look up, but I saw that everyone was being helped, so I returned to my other work. This is not an excuse, it is how it happened.

I was very busy this entire week, and got a lot of work done. In fact, I felt that I was particularly efficient yesterday. I worked the front desk when necessary, and often work it more than anyone else because I rarely take breaks. I will send you the required daily message listing my work for the day. If you insist on putting your message in my personnel file, then I ask that you place this response there as well.

Thank you,

Allie

Figure 7.6: Ineffective E-mail – Employee to Supervisor

Now ask yourself, what did the employee do right? What did they do wrong? Allie, if she disagrees, seems within her rights to respectfully tell her supervisor how the situation differs from what the manager observed. The beginning of her reply, pointing out what

---

[16] Here is another example of where this text book is written in a very casual format. However, notes like this are designed to get you thinking about the subject matter, thus there is a reason to what may seem to be less than technical language.

she has done well in the past, was good. However, there are some serious issues with this reply.

First, the subject line is a bit abrupt, bordering on disrespectful. Also, the closing, "thank you", does not seem appropriate to the content of the message. The overall tone of the message seems a little angry, almost belligerent. One main issue is that Allie needs to read the original message more carefully. The manager ended by writing, "this notice will not be placed in your Official Personnel File." Allie misread it, and in her reply said that the manager "insisted" on putting the note in the file. Allie argued over a point that was positive in her favor, and she showed herself to be a callous reader, misunderstanding what she reads. Allie let her anger rush her response.

When you get an upsetting e-mail, you need to read it, then close it. Then read it again a few minutes or hours later, after you calm down. Then write a response and save it as a draft. Finally, read the response again some time later, ensuring that it is appropriate and being careful to remove any angry language.

Following are ten basic guidelines to help you write effective, responsive e-mail messages:

1. Never write in anger.
2. Use descriptive subject lines.
3. Identify yourself clearly.
4. Carefully choose words that convey your intended tone.
5. Keep the message concise, focused, and readable.
6. Write professionally in language, content, and style.
7. Be certain of your facts.
8. Use attachments only when necessary, and introduce them in the document.
9. Do not assume privacy.
10. Specifically state any action that you are requesting and whether you require a reply.

## Summary

Resumes, cover letters, and e-mail are all types of correspondence that many of us write and send regularly. For each, format and content varies and is highly personal. But also for each, it is important to write in a way that is easy for the reader, both in form and content. Be concise, clear. and grammatically correct.

## Additional Readings: Suggested Job Search Texts

Bolles, R.N. (2006). What color is your parachute? 2007: A practical manual for job-hunters and career-changers. Berkeley, CA: Ten Speed Press.

> This is a well-written, even entertaining, text that provides excellent information on how to find a job. It includes specifics on job-hunting, making a career change, excelling in interviews, and more.

Bennett, S. (2005). The elements of resume style: Essential rules and eye-opening advice for writing resumes and cover letters that work. New York: American Management Association.

This text offers excellent tips, tricks, and guidelines for developing effective resumes and cover letters. Many excellent samples are given.

# CHAPTER 8

# Oral Communications and Graphics

*Speech is a mirror of the soul: as a man speaks, so is he.*
*~Publilius Syrus*

## Chapter 8: Oral Communications and Graphics

### Introduction

Technical communications has many facets, and it is not all about written words. Pictures, photos, tables, charts, and various graphics can be used to aid communications, as can body language and speech patterns. But even these other forms of graphical or live communications can benefit from what we have discussed so far. Most computer science, information technology, engineering, and business professionals will be called upon at some time to give or participate in an oral presentation (whether live, tele-conference, or video conference); thus the ability to present oneself well is important. In a live presentation in front of a group, you need to know your audience, what they are like, what they know, and what they need to know. You need to understand the purpose of your presentation or speech, and you need to present yourself and your information in a credible, intelligent, well organized, way so as to be certain your audience understands you. If you understand and know these things about your audience, you can then communicate well, verbally and graphically.

### Oral Communications

To communicate effectively in a live situation, remember what you have read throughout this text. Be clear. Be concise. Speak to your audience. And before you even begin, develop a plan and create a rough draft (for oral presentations, this means write notes or a speech, then practice it). If you plan, practice and understand your content well, you will do just fine. When addressing a live audience, remember the following basics:

- Dress appropriately to the audience, location, and topic.
- Prepare ahead of time; have notes.
- Familiarize yourself with the room you will be in, as well as the facilities and equipment of the room.
- Rehearse what you will say. This will help with both your content and your pacing.
- Do not speak too quickly.
- Speak well and in a confident manner.
- Project your voice, as necessary, depending upon the room and audio equipment.
- Use visuals, if necessary, to punctuate what you say and add content.
- Memorize what you will say and refer to your notes only occasionally. Do not read, word-for-word, from your notes. Do not simply read your slides.
- Make eye contact with audience members. If this is difficult for you, try focusing just above the eyes of the audience. Try to look from person to person to engage everyone.
- Be sensitive to your audience. If they appear bored with a specific segment of your presentation, put a new spin on it or move on. Keep them engaged.
- Avoid nervous gestures and unnecessary movement.
- Invite questions, and never dismiss a question as unworthy or make any audience member feel uncomfortable.

Take a moment and consider a recent speech or presentation that you witnessed. Perhaps there was a presentation at work, or maybe you saw a political figure giving a speech on television. Think about that oral communication, then consider the following questions:

- What things did the speaker do to make themselves appear credible?
- What else might they have done to increase their credibility?
- What did the speaker do to capture and hold the audience's attention? What more could they have done?
- Did the person use phrases like "ummm" or "like," or nervous gestures that detracted from their message?
- Does the speaker obviously read from a cue-card? Or did they have their speech memorized?

Use your thoughts on these questions to consider your own past, or future, oral presentations. Remember in past speeches that you have viewed or listened to how both the good and the bad impacted you as an audience. Consider how you can use this information to improve your own speaking in the future. While as a writer you can learn much about your own writing by reviewing the work of others, similarly you can learn much about improving your own oral communications by watching and considering the speeches of others.

## Using Graphics Effectively

Now let's consider graphical aids in both live and written presentations. Live presentations often include slideshows. These are both a way of sharing information and of keeping the viewers' attention. One mistake many presenters make is to show slides, then read them word-for-word. This is a quick way to lose your audience and is not effective. Many audience members find this insulting, almost as though the presenter feels they are incapable of reading for themselves. When you develop slides, use graphics when possible and add text only to emphasize important points. Use interesting, brief phrases in large, readable fonts.

Graphics, especially in documents, are often overlooked as less important features, even afterthoughts. This is usually a mistake. Illustrations are very important parts of a document; they can be used to clarify, simplify, summarize, attract attention, drive a point home, and even conserve space in a document. However, like many other aspects of communications, graphics should be used when they will enhance a document, not added just for the sake of adding them. Some documents do not require graphics and would not benefit from them, and that is fine. But many documents are well served by judiciously placed tables, pictures, and drawings.

Graphics can be valuable tools in written communications, particularly in documents such as instructions. If you have recently bought a computer, you may have noticed that most new computers come with a simple poster-type set of instructions that graphically show how to set up your computer. In addition, the back of the computer is color coded and has pictures to help the user plug the correct peripherals in the correct place. It is nearly impossible not to know where to put the mouse — the green end of the mouse goes to the green circle on the back of the computer, which also has a little picture of a mouse underneath it. Imagine how much money this little addition of color and graphics must save computer companies in help desk calls. Similarly, video game and stereo instructions often come with directions that are almost entirely composed of illustrations, showing what connects to what; you barely have to read a word. These are effective uses of graphics.

We use visuals to communicate every day. When you are driving, you do not know to stop simply because you see the word STOP on a sign. Chances are you recognize the large, red octagon and know to stop long before you actually see the individual letters. You go to a family restaurant and in addition to text describing each food item, there is a tempting picture. You drive down the road and are bombarded with billboards mixing text and graphics. The use of visual aids in our society is so prolific that you probably don't even realize how often you rely on pictures rather than spoken or written words to make a certain impression upon you. This can be true for documents as well.

You have all seen pie-charts used to depict ratios, and certainly these are more effective than simply listing ratios and quantities. A pie-chart can be understood at a glance, much more quickly and clearly than mere words. Even a bulleted list is similar to a graphic, in that it logically presents information in an easy-to-read format in the same manner as a pie-chart, bar graphs, or similar graphics. Tables are often used as space-saving devices, allowing columns to line up and much information to be presented, again, at a glance and in an easy-to-read format. Photographs, drawings, word art, and other figures all can be used to accomplish the number one goal of a document – to be readable for the audience.

Let's take a look at one example. Perhaps you are writing a research paper on Internet and computer use in the United States. You have written a paragraph that reads:

> Computer use, particularly Internet use, in the United States is rising at a steady rate. As of 2000 only 20% of Americans had a computer in their home. However, in 2007 over 50% of Americans have a home computer. Similarly, in 2000 only 10% of Americans had regular access to the Internet, either at home, school or work, whereas in 2007 nearly 70% of Americans have access in one of these three places.

After you read that paragraph, did you remember all of those figures? With all of those numbers and boring sentences, did you even get the main idea of the paragraph? Perhaps, as that was a simple paragraph, but think if the numbers were even more complicated, and if more ideas were presented. Conversely, consider the same information, but presented in graphics form in Figure 8.1, on the following page.

Computer use, particularly Internet use, in the United States is rising at a steady rate, as depicted in the following graphs:

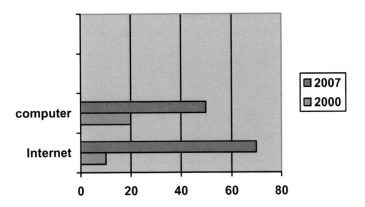

computer – Percentage of Americans with computers at home
Internet –   Percentage of Americans with Internet access at home, work or school

Figure 8.1: Computer and Internet Use

This chart provides a quick, at a glance overview of the percentage of Americans with computer and Internet access, with minimal writing to read. This is much easier to take in than the previous paragraph.

When using graphics in academic and professional writing, the following general guidelines will add to the effectiveness of the graphic:

- Place graphics near the text they are modifying.
- Allow ample white space within and around the graphic to allow it to be readable, but not so much that it appears lost and alone on the page.
- Use color when possible and appropriate.
- Always give every graphic a figure number and name, placed just above or below the graphic.
- Refer the reader directly to every graphic from within the text. Graphics that are thrown in without reference are often not looked at, or are ineffective, as they lack context.
- Ensure that graphic resolution is sufficient to be attractive and easily readable.
- Cite the source, just after the title, if it has been borrowed or adapted from another.

With careful consideration and planning, graphics can be an excellent way to add interest and meaning to written documentation.

**Summary**

Technical communication generally brings to mind writing, but it also includes the use of graphical representations and oral communications. The same basic tenants of good communications apply equally to all of these types of communications. Remember your audience, be clear, be concise, and present yourself in a credible, ethical manner, and your communications, whatever the form, will be effective.

# References

Ballard, R. (1989). *The discovery of the Titanic*. Toronto: Madison Press Books.

Columbia Accident Investigation Board (CAIB). (2003). CAIB Report. Retrieved April 2, 2007 from, http://spaceflight.nasa.gov/shuttle/archives/sts-107/investigation/index.html

Earle, S. C. (1919). The theory and practice of technical writing. London, England: MacMillan.

Gruchawka, S. (2006). TechDeepWeb.com. Retrieved April 2, 2007 from www.TechDeepWeb.com

information. (2007). American Heritage Dictionary.

Jankowski, M. (2007). Migrating to Microsoft Windows Vista: Technical reference [unpublished].

Mainelli, T. (May 2004). 64-bit universe expands. *PC World*, 34.

Nua Internet Surveys. (April, 2003). More high-speed Net subscribers in US. Retrieved March 28, 2004 from, http://www.nua.ie/surveys/.

Pei, M. (1900). Invitation to linguistics. New York: Doubleday & Company, Inc.

Rogers Commission. (1986). Report of the Presidential Commission on the Space Shuttle Challenger Accident. Retrieved April 2, 2007 from, http://history.nasa.gov/rogersrep/v1ch1.htm

Snarski, M. (2007). Cover Letter. [unpublished].

United Press International and American Heritage Magazine [compilers]. (1964). *Four days: The historical record of the death of President Kennedy*. New York: American Heritage Publishing Co., Inc.

United States Government. (1776). Declaration of Independence.

Wilson, E.B., Jr. (1952). An introduction to scientific research. New York: McGraw-Hill, Inc.